FEVER PITCH

THE RISE OF THE
PREMIER LEAGUE
1992-2004

PAUL McCARTHY

SPHERE

SPHERE

First published in Great Britain in 2022 by Sphere

1 3 5 7 9 10 8 6 4 2

A CIP catalogue record for this book
is available from the British Library.

Hardback ISBN: 978-1-4087-2717-1
Trade paperback ISBN: 978-1-4087-2718-8

Typeset in Sabon by M Rules
Printed and bound in Great Britain by Clays Ltd, Elcograf S.p.A.

Papers used by Sphere are from well-managed forests
and other responsible sources.

Sphere
An imprint of
Little, Brown Book Group
Carmelite House
50 Victoria Embankment
London EC4Y 0DZ

An Hachette UK Company
www.hachette.co.uk

www.littlebrown.co.uk

FEVER PITCH

The Premier League has been a huge part of my life for the past thirty years but never came close to being the most important part. That role has been played by my wonderful wife, Lisa and our two fantastic kids, Sophie and Joe. Thank you for always being there.

CONTENTS

FOREWORD: ALAN SHEARER

Thirty years, where did they all go?

When you talk about three decades of the Premier League, it feels like it should be in the dim and distant past, but to me it's still so vivid that it could be yesterday. You think back to those key moments in your life – leaving Southampton for Blackburn as the most expensive player in Britain and then joining Newcastle as the most expensive player in the world – and it feels so fresh in my mind.

As a player, all you want to do is get out there on a Saturday afternoon and win games, you don't think about politics, money, boardroom chatter; it's all about the match and the fans. But when the Premier League started in 1992, even the players recognised the significance. Something important had changed – and it felt exciting.

I'll certainly never forget my first Premier League game; it was my debut for Blackburn, and I scored twice against Crystal Palace. I woke up the next morning knowing this was the start of a fantastic journey.

I have to smile to myself when I look back at the footage of that first season, in fact, those first few years. The state of the pitches, they were dreadful! Recently I walked across the pitch at St Mary's Stadium in Southampton with Gary Neville and Micah Richards and it was like the most luxuriant carpet you could buy. As I said to Gary, imagine how many goals I would have scored if the ball hadn't been bobbling all over the place back in our day!

When you are making those kinds of comparisons, you realise just how far the Premier League has come in those thirty years. The grounds are magnificent, the facilities for fans are wonderful and the whole experience of match days is light years from when the league started. When I was going to sign for Blackburn, Kenny Dalglish, Jack Walker and Ray Harford didn't want me to visit Ewood Park because it was so ramshackle; they thought I'd change my mind.

Now the Premier League is a global phenomenon in so many different ways. I am very fortunate to travel around the world through football and the recognition our game gets thanks to the overseas coverage is, at times, astonishing and the love for the Premier League is undeniable.

So much has changed for the players, too. Yes, wages are fantastic, we can't deny that, but it's the technical side of the game that has improved, the ability to play with the greatest players in the world has brought out the very best in the English game. I remember the season we won the title with Blackburn, there was only Henning Berg and Robbie Slater who came from overseas; now you can have half a dozen different languages in a single dressing room.

Would I have swapped my time in the Premier League to play now? It's a question I get asked a lot and the answer is always 'no'. I was part of something special, something exciting and invigorating. I was there when the Premier League was new, when 'Alive and Kicking' was its anthem and we were pioneers of sorts. That's something I would never swap or want to lose.

Alan Shearer CBE DL

1

Talking About a Revolution

The napkin is now kept in an airtight bag for safety. Really, it should have a home in a football museum or, at the very least, be on display at the Premier League's London HQ. Instead, David Dein guards and protects it, this six-inch square of paper covered in slightly spidery handwriting, the blue ink just beginning to fade.

With the required sense of solemnity, the former Arsenal vice-chairman presents it as you might an ancient artefact. In football terms, perhaps it is one. For this is the document that revolutionised the game, a blueprint for transformation that dismantled a century of accepted thinking and forced football into the Modern Age.

We are travelling west out of London Waterloo and have barely hit the suburbs when he proffers the Ziploc in my direction. 'Do you know what that is?' he asks, confident that I won't have a clue. 'It's the first draft of the Founders' Agreement for the Premier League, the way the league was going to be set up, how the money was to be divided – all on a paper napkin I had to hand when we first decided something had to change.'

The 'we' was Dein, the driving force behind change at Arsenal; his North London equivalent, Irving Scholar at

Tottenham Hotspur; the Manchester United chairman, Martin Edwards, and the Merseyside pair of Noel White from Liverpool and Philip Carter at Everton. In the late eighties and early nineties, these were the 'Big Five' – a group of clubs who knew that without a seismic change, football was on a slow dive towards mediocrity. Exile from Europe post-Heysel had seen standards fall on the pitch, while facilities within grounds were an insult to fans. Add the blight of hooliganism and the significant fall in attendances, and football had become a pariah sport in the eyes of the Government and large parts of society.

Today, Dein uses the napkin as a prop on his numerous visits to prisons, part of his role in the Twinning Project, a charity he helped set up with the aim of rehabilitating offenders through football. More than thirty years ago that napkin was the impetus behind the birth of the Premier League, a land-grab that shook the game to its foundations and would ultimately lead to the former powerbrokers of the Football Association and the Football League becoming subservient, hapless onlookers.

Football's Magna Carta had actually been drawn up in November 1990 at a dinner on London's South Bank, but its seeds were sown five years earlier by a series of tragedies. On 11 May 1985, fifty-six fans lost their lives and almost three hundred were injured in an inferno at Bradford City's Valley Parade ground when a cigarette fell on to accumulated rubbish below a virtually decrepit wooden stand which was soon engulfed in flames.

On the same day, fighting between Birmingham City and Leeds United fans at St Andrew's led to a wall collapsing, crushing a fifteen-year-old schoolboy, Ian Hambridge, who later died of his head injuries. Less than three weeks later, thirty-nine people died at the Heysel Stadium in Belgium after violent clashes between Liverpool and Juventus fans, again causing the collapse of a wall in a stadium which an investigation would conclude was not fit for purpose.

Yet, while football as a whole seemingly refused either to listen or to learn from these horrific lessons, there was a realisation among the Big Five that the authorities were presiding over a decline of a sport that may have been slow, but was ultimately irreversible. The likes of Dein, Edwards and Scholar were, first and foremost, smart businessmen who had run major companies of their own and who knew their way around a balance sheet, were comfortable with the process of profit projection and margins, and saw there needed to be a sea change in both the structure and the thinking at the heart of the game. A ninety-two-club decision-making model was unwieldly and benefited reactionary thinking to the point where Dein's proposal for putting the names of players as well as numbers on the back of shirts was denied as some clubs 'would not have enough laundry room'. In the face of this recalcitrance, an alliance was formed.

As Martin Edwards explains, 'I became Manchester United chairman in 1980, David joined the Arsenal board a little bit after that and Irving Scholar took over Tottenham in 1982. We were all very similar football nuts. We were all dead keen. I think we all realised that under the ninety-two-club Football League formula, the big clubs in England were never really going to reach their full, full potential.

'When I took over United, my big ambition was to catch Liverpool, because Liverpool were the dominant club in England. But once you achieve that, you think, "OK, we're capable of winning the League, we're capable of being successful, now, who do you want to compete against?" And you look at Real Madrid, Barcelona, Bayern Munich, and you think, "How are we going to be able to compete with them?"

And the only way you're able to compete with them is if you're getting more worth.

'Yet all clubs were equal in terms of voting rights, all clubs were equal in terms of television revenue. We all got £25,000, even though it was us who were appearing on television most of the time. You also had to put a percentage of your gate revenue into the central pot, which I can understand if you're sharing it with twenty or twenty-two other clubs but not with ninety-two clubs.'

With a shared ambition of autonomy, talks between the like-minded Edwards, Dein and Scholar began in 1985 and expanded to include White and Carter from Merseyside who, while more traditional in their outlook, still recognised the need for change in exactly the same way and gladly threw in their lot with the thrusting reformers. However, it took the dreadful events of Hillsborough four years later to galvanise their collective determination.

The deaths of ninety-five innocent fans on 15 April 1989 (two more were to die in later years) changed societal attitudes towards football. It forced the game into a reckoning which it had avoided for too long. Supporters were often treated like cattle, herded into grounds that lacked even the most basic facilities, told they had no voice, their pleas for something approaching civility contemptuously ignored by the game's authorities. Even clubs who actually wanted to improve their stadium were hamstrung by a lack of both funds and vision, a relic of a sport that saw change as an anathema and the preservation of the status quo as a given.

Justice for the families of the ninety-seven may have had to wait thirty years, but football could not afford a second's delay. Prime Minister Margaret Thatcher faced down football's authorities. She demanded that every fan should carry an identity card, a plan rejected by the FA, the Football

League and the police. There was to be no denying Thatcher's next move, however: a full investigation headed by Lord Justice Peter Taylor. In the space of thirty-one days, the Taylor Report did more to change the game than any other intervention since the formation of the FA in 1863.

The requirement from Taylor for all-seater stadia meant the single biggest investment project ever undertaken by the top two English divisions. Government and local authority grants barely softened the financial blow; assistance from the FA only scratched the surface. And television revenue? It amounted to next to nothing if, for example, in the case of Manchester United, redeveloping the Stretford End alone came with a bill of £10 million. A four-year rights deal with ITV signed in 1988 may have been worth £44 million, but divided – albeit weighted towards the top flight – by ninety-two clubs meant the Big Five and the remainder of the old First Division were faced with the kind of crippling bills few could accommodate.

Even the euphoria of England's World Cup campaign at Italia 90 did nothing to dilute the financial burden. Bobby Robson's team may have lifted a nation with their charge to the semi-finals before exiting on penalties to West Germany. Paul Gascoigne may have emerged as a totemic symbol of gallant defeat. And, yes, a combination of sunshine and Ecstasy had seen a transformation in the face of the typical England fan from snarling hooligan to (largely) loved-up raver. But there was no significant benefit to the bottom line. The 1990–91 season saw a rise in attendances in the old First Division as fans who had previously stayed away wanted to experience this new feel-good factor. That rise included the welcome sight of more women and families attending matches, just the market football at the highest level had always sought to tap. But while the demand was there, the Taylor Report's determination that whole stands and sections of the ground had to be closed for all-seater renovation meant this new influx of support did not come close to shifting the financial dial for clubs still struggling to pay the bills.

Enter Greg Dyke. Often bullish and belligerent, Dyke had made the move from newspaper journalism into television and, having helped revitalise the fortunes of ITV's TV-am, was now the senior executive at London Weekend Television. For a man who would go on to become the chairman of the FA, Dyke held that institution and the Football League in healthy contempt, recognising an unsustainability in the existing model both as a businessman and as a fan of Brentford (albeit with an allegiance to Manchester United that would latterly see him join the Old Trafford board). Instinctively, Dyke sensed there was more than just a move to implement change at the top of the game; it was fast becoming a tidal wave – and one that he believed ITV could surf. That belief was to prove short lived.

Dyke had already found a kindred spirit in Dein, with whom he had negotiated ITV's £44 million broadcast contract in 1988. Now he did his best to galvanise the Gang of Five, dropping ever heavier hints that if there was truly a desire to rip up the accepted order of things, ITV would be happy to spearhead from a broadcast angle. 'We were facing up to the challenge of the Taylor Report,' admits Dein. 'We'd always been talking, going back to the mid eighties, asking ourselves, "How are we going to change the game?" Then Greg came on to the scene and he gave us impetus. He gave us courage, I have to say, and the whole thing fell into place.'

It was Dyke who hosted the dinner on 16 November 1990 in LWT's headquarters overlooking the Thames. Nobody can seem to remember what was on the menu except revolution. The Big Five finally crystallised a thought process half-a-decade in the making, with Dein jotting down notes on his now precious napkin.

Emboldened by the positive direction of travel, Dyke upped the ante after the meeting. He wrote to the Big Five clubs, offering them £1 million each for the exclusive broadcast rights to their matches. At the November dinner, a putative figure of £750,000 had been discussed – and certainly not discounted by the clubs – and Dyke sensed increasing the offer would add even more volition to the process. He wasn't wrong.

The Big Five approached Rick Parry to take on the role of chief executive of the proposed new league. Parry had been a lead figure in Manchester's failed bid for the 1992 Olympics and had impressed with his drive, vision and credibility. Convincing the Liverpool fan to leave a senior position at consultancy giants Ernst & Young proved to be easier than Dein, Edwards and company expected. It also gave the clubs an element of protection, with Parry their fireguard providing a degree of deniability should news of their plotting leak. Incredibly, it never did, an indication of just how little even a ravenous media expected anything to change within football.

So, while the breakaway clubs had crossed the Rubicon, strengthened by a guaranteed million pounds a year (when Arsenal's annual turnover amounted to £1.5 million compared to something just short of £400 million today), there were still a thousand steps to take. As much as the money thrilled, there was no appetite for a closed shop of five teams playing against each other up to eight times a year. The net had to be cast wider.

Dein recalls, 'We thought to ourselves, "So how do we get the others on board?" And we thought, "Well, you know, if we get ten clubs, the other twelve will come." So, we all decided to have one dancing partner each, the ones who had traditionally sided with us on major decisions. I think mine was West Ham, somebody else had Newcastle, somebody else had Sheffield Wednesday. And so on.

'Then it would be, "How are you doing? How's your partner? Yeah, we're okay, I think we're okay." Then when we actually had ten clubs signed up, we knew the other twelve would come along because that's what they tended to do. That's exactly what happened.'

But it was a far from straightforward process, no matter how blithely Dein explains it away. The dance partners were wary, scared of missing out on an opportunity but equally terrified of a misstep and the ramifications of such a momentous move. Up and down the country, hotel rooms were booked anonymously as White, Carter and Edwards courted their northern allies, while Dein and Scholar networked assiduously in London and the south.

Secrecy and confidentiality were key, although that sometimes went out the window. Rick Parry recalls a meeting with Edwards in a hotel in Manchester where a suite was booked under the name of Martin & Company. Arriving at the hotel reception, Parry asked for directions to the suite, only for the receptionist to reply in all innocence, 'Oh, you must be here for the Manchester United meeting, then.'

For four months, the mutineers, revolutionaries – call them what you will – took the message out to the First Division clubs that they could be masters of their own destiny, that a new age beckoned for anybody with a vision for an improved, streamlined football pyramid that would never again be held back by the reactionaries clinging on to power, the-big-man-in-a-small-town mentality desperate to avoid a change that might threaten their position.

It was a tantalising prospect for many, but still the overriding question was: what would be the backlash from the game's authorities when, inevitably, secrecy gave way to a public statement of intent? What would the FA and the Football League do?

The answer, for the FA at least, was roll over and have its tummy tickled.

History has not been kind to Graham Kelly. Speaking personally, I found him hugely likeable away from the cameras, microphones and notebooks, the kind of man who was happy to be dumped in goal when playing for the England press team during Euro 96 despite holding the role of FA chief executive at the time. To be fair, he was far from the worst goalkeeper the press team has ever had.

But as an administrator and executive, he will always carry the scar of Hillsborough happening on his watch, haunted by a series of floundering missteps around England managerial appointments and sackings. A measure of his often tone-deaf approach to the demands of the job was illustrated when a handful of chief football writers were holed up in a hotel in Marseille's old port watching the streets of the city set alight as English, French and Algerian thugs fought running battles, setting cars on fire and smashing windows in restaurants and bars before retreating from baton-wielding police.

It was a horrific sight, the kind that too often blighted England's travels in Europe. Calls were made to the FA asking for a reaction, when suddenly we spotted Kelly sitting in the hotel bar just yards away, watching Jamaica v Croatia on television. Incredulous, a couple of us approached him and, pointing to the carnage just a few hundred yards away, politely enquired what the actual hell he was planning to do – only to be informed there would 'probably' be a press conference in the morning. Hardly inspiring.

Yet arguably the worst error of Kelly's nine-year reign at the FA was the way he ceded authority to the breakaway clubs driving what had become known as the Premier League. Perhaps it was due to the traditional enmity between the FA and the Football League, a battle between the 'blazers' and the clubs, both sides jostling for supremacy, both believing THEY were charged with control of the game's soul. Little did they realise the events of early 1991 would see both their positions diminished irrevocably within a decade.

Previously, Kelly had served eleven years at the Football League as secretary, so he would have been attuned to the mood among the leading clubs even if he may not have been aware of how deep-rooted their plans to rip up the established order were. Having 'crossed the floor' to the FA in 1989, he was the obvious first port of call for the conspirators as they tested the water. If they were expecting any kind of reluctance on behalf of Kelly and the FA, those thoughts were dispelled in the very first meeting between the chief executive, Dein and White in December 1990.

It became clear they shared much common ground with Kelly who, at the time, was preparing his own blueprint for the future of the English game. That particular plan foresaw an era where the biggest clubs, as the major revenue drivers through television rights deals and other commercial ventures, would demand a louder and stronger voice in the way the game was run. In Kelly's opinion, as long as the FA maintained alignment with the clubs and, titularly at least, had their name over the door, it was a natural and acceptable progression.

Buoyed by Kelly's willingness to, in Dein's words, 'open the door a little' for their venture, the next step was to march through it waving a battle plan for the breakaway and a proposal of its structure to the FA. However jubilant the mood among the plotters, they still faced the prospect of a battle with the Football League who, under the leadership of its

President, Bill Fox, were not about to allow for the destruction of their 102-year-old bastion by five slick-suited upstarts.

Fox, in particular, rattled his sabre louder than anybody, determined to fight every inch of the way to prevent any change but, as Dein explains, 'I don't want to talk badly of Bill. He was the chairman of Blackburn Rovers and he was, "You know it's always been like this for a hundred years. You can't change it now." Well, a hundred years ago buses were drawn by horses, now we've got electric cars so that's what he had to deal with.'

The one weapon the League did have was its Articles of Association, which stated that any member club seeking to resign was forced to give three years' notice. In the past, this had been the perceived stumbling block when the Big Five – and others – were contemplating the kind of revolution that was now potentially weeks away.

But if Fox thought that was going to be a deterrent, then he had seriously misjudged and underestimated the mood of revolt. 'We didn't have the luxury of three years,' Dein recalls. 'We had clubs going up and down, it wouldn't be the same group of clubs and we couldn't afford to wait, we were hot to trot, we had to nail it.

'Fortunately, we had a very astute barrister, Mark Phillips, together with Rick Parry who was the CEO designate, when Mark had what he calls his "eureka" moment. He was in his study one day with the Football League rules in one hand and the FA rules in the other and they weren't compatible. The League rules said three years' notice of resignation, the FA's said one year's notice. So, we resigned under the FA rules.'

A statement of some simplicity but a situation of intense legal scrutiny. The FA were accused by the League of acting in an 'arbitrary and undemocratic' way, risking endangering the very safety of the English game for an 'illusion'.

On 8 April 1991 all twenty-two First Division clubs met at the FA's Lancaster Gate headquarters. Dein, Edwards, Scholar, White and Carter – that original Gang of Five – were joined by the likes of Chelsea's Ken Bates and Dave Richards from Sheffield Wednesday, who had been convinced this was not only a significant step forward but an essential one if the game was to survive. Already English football was being plundered by its European neighbours, with star names like Chris Waddle having departed for Marseille in 1989 to be followed by David Platt to Bari later that year and Paul Gascoigne, the absolute jewel in the crown of the England team, unable to resist the riches and siren call of Serie A when Lazio came calling. Even defenders like Des Walker were a target for Italy and would leave for Sampdoria the following year. The talent drain left English clubs even less competitive every time Europe opened its chequebook, and in the eyes of the clubs most at risk, only the dramatic transformation of the league could end that.

Five years out of European competitions (with an extra year's ban for Liverpool) had seen English clubs fall light years behind their continental rivals. Scholar estimated the Italian, Spanish and French leagues were all a far more attractive proposition to the best players in the world and that the talent drain would become a torrent unless decisive action was taken. It was an argument that easily carried the day for any club that might still have possessed a scintilla of doubt.

Of course, there was still some horse-trading to be done. The original plan, and one sanctioned by Kelly and the FA, was for an eighteen-team Premier League, but that was diluted to include all the current First Division clubs, with the acceptance that relegation and promotion remained sacrosanct. Ironically, Bill Fox's Blackburn would benefit from the extended group, securing promotion from the old Second

Division to become a founder of the Premier League. Sadly, Fox passed away before he could see his club transformed.

With the resignation of twenty-two clubs now backed and rubber-stamped by the FA, the fight transferred from oak-panelled offices to the High Court. On 17 July, the clubs signed a Founder Members' Agreement which saw the Football League take the inevitable step of legal action. The shrewd legal instincts of Mark Phillips proved correct: the High Court decided the ultimate governance of the game rested with the FA and with that decision, the Premier League was no longer a pipe dream of five men with a sense of purpose, it was reality.

Despite defeat in the courts, the Football League's resentment was palpable – visceral, even. So much so that all ninety-two clubs were called to a meeting at the Grand Connaught Rooms in London on 23 September where it was left to the FA's then Administration Manager, Pat Smith, to explain the reasoning behind her organisation's decision to facilitate the destruction of a structure that had stood for more than a century. Standing on a chair so she could be both seen and heard, Smith calmly explained that, rather than selling the game's soul, it was better the FA were able to control this breakaway group than be railroaded by it.

Smith's explanation was grudgingly accepted across the board but the animosity survives even to this day – not that the FA or Football League can do a thing about it. Perhaps now both bodies share the sentiment of legendary football scribe Brian Glanville, who wrote in the *Sunday Times* that we were witnessing the birth of the 'Greed is Good' league. Given the astonishing success, and often excess, of the Premier League thirty years later, it's difficult to disagree.

Cruelly, one of the first victims of the Premier League was the man who surely provided the catalyst for it. Greg Dyke's

ITV bid £200 million over four years for the broadcast rights and received the backing of four of the original Big Five. In different times, loyalty to Dyke might have been paramount; instead, Rupert Murdoch stuck an extra £100 million on the table and Dyke was just another who found himself chewed up and spat out by clubs who had quite literally written their own rules to get this far and were never going to be afraid of writing more.

Perhaps Dein sums it up most succinctly. 'Football wanted to keep the family together but the family had outgrown the house. That is the truth.'

2

A Man for All Seasons

The word had come from the very top. There was only one shot the Sky cameras had to get. And so, when the final whistle blew, they swung towards the Old Trafford directors' box to capture the image of Sir Matt Busby, walking stick in hand, beaming smile on his face, singing along to 'Always Look on the Bright Side of Life' in time with forty thousand euphoric Manchester United fans. Only when the cameras had lingered long enough on Sir Matt did they cut back to events on the pitch and the man who had inspired scenes of such rapture.

It would be the last time in his Old Trafford career that Alex Ferguson was forced to accept second billing to anybody at the Theatre of Dreams.

The shadow of Busby, the one that had proved too daunting and overwhelming for every one of Ferguson's predecessors, had been lifted. The title, which had eluded United for twenty-six years, since the days of Charlton, Best and Law, was back in Manchester and Ferguson's own seven years of frustration were at an end. Fittingly, the first season of the Premier League era had crowned a man who would go on to become arguably its most influential figure.

Sure, smart men in suits drove the Premier League's inception, an acquiescent FA may have rubber-stamped it and Rupert Murdoch most certainly funded it, but it was Ferguson who lived it, embodied it, personified all its drama and its ability to deify and destroy in equal measure.

His dominance of the Premier League, not just in those early years but until his retirement two decades after that initial triumph, saw him transform English football and the way it was viewed – and sold – around the world. Without Ferguson's United, the Premier League would have been successful, but even the likes of former chief executive Richard Scudamore concede its global significance may not have been quite as assured.

Speaking to journalists at a private lunch to celebrate the League's tenth anniversary, Scudamore revealed that if there was a difficult negotiation to be faced, be it with broadcasting rights or a commercial partner, his secret weapon was always Ferguson. A word, a handshake, a conversation with him would so often end any stalemate or ease open a door that seemed firmly shut. It was a power of presence and personality that none have matched.

And yet, by the standards of the current Premier League era, Ferguson would have considered himself fortunate even to be in a job at United, let alone usher in a period of utter domination. From his appointment in November 1986 through to 1992 when United stumbled to second place behind Leeds United, Ferguson had underwhelmed and only the boardroom support of Busby and chairman Martin Edwards had saved him.

Ten trophies with Aberdeen and the end of Glasgow's dominance of Scottish football meant nothing to United fans starved of title glory and, worse, seeing red and blue on Merseyside carving up the League between them throughout the eighties. An FA Cup victory in 1990 was a mere salve; European success in the Cup Winners' Cup a year later helped, but, as Edwards points out, it was considered the barest of minimums for United even if it pointed to an upwards trajectory.

'We'd gone so long without winning the League it became like a monster hanging over us. Every year that went by it got more and more difficult and the tension grew. As far as Alex is concerned, I can't see clubs being that patient these days. Liverpool were reasonably patient with Jürgen Klopp before he won the title but generally people are looking for immediate, instant success.

'We used to receive a lot of letters from supporters complaining that Alex wasn't the right man. He'd come from Scotland; he hadn't got experience in the English League, and all the rest of it. All you could ever do was write back and explain about all the hard work that was going on behind the scenes and that we were developing the youth team and just be patient and it will all come right in the end. But of course, supporters are looking for immediate results; they're judging it on every Saturday. And if results aren't going well, they become impatient.'

Impatience barely covered it; mutiny was a far more apt description. It reached a nadir on 9 December 1989, the day Ferguson still describes as his 'darkest hour'. Trailing 2–1 at home to Crystal Palace, a ripple went through the Old Trafford crowd as 33,000 supporters were alerted to a banner that had been unfurled:

3 years of excuses and it's still crap. Ta ra Fergie.

A murmur became applause, became a roar of appreciation and agreement and saw the architect of the protest earn his own place in United's folklore. Pete Molyneux had been a fan for twenty-six years; in 1989 he had reached the stage where frustration had turned to anger. As he explains, 'The football wasn't good, we'd scored the lowest number of goals since the relegation season of 1974 and Ferguson had spent a lot of money.

'Manchester United fans expect to see their team try and play attractive football, expansive, attacking football; to go forward at power and pace. And if we're getting that we can live with being second or third or fourth and hope that we're moving in the right direction. But around that time Fergie's football was dire, it was really poor and not adventurous enough, not enough goals. You put up with it for a while, but some fans would vote with their feet.

'I couldn't not go, I was in love with the club and the manager is separate from that, he's just the present incumbent. So, bit by bit, I suppose, I fell out of love with him. Like a marriage, it comes to a point where you decide if you're going to divorce or not and I didn't want a divorce from the club, but I wanted a divorce from the manager.'

But the decree nisi would have to wait. FA Cup victory over Crystal Palace after a replay gave Ferguson some breathing space, followed by a European Cup Winners' Cup triumph against Barcelona in Rotterdam that reignited the spark of a European dream that had laid dormant since Busby's time twenty-three years before. The following season came Ferguson's third piece of silverware: the League Cup, thanks to a Brian McClair winner against Nottingham Forest at Wembley. While Ferguson's touch in cup competitions was golden, all it did was temporarily disguise the gnawing ache of missing out on the prize all United fans demanded – the League title.

The 1991–92 season, the last of its kind under the wizened hand of the Football League, should have been the year United ended the wait. The club had invested heavily in the transfer market over the previous three years, breaking the

British transfer fee record when paying Middlesbrough £2.3 million for Gary Pallister, as well as bringing in established internationals in Paul Ince, Neil Webb, Paul Parker and Mike Phelan. Ferguson had also gone some way to reversing the exodus towards continental Europe by bringing in Peter Schmeichel from Danish side Brondby and paying Shakhtar Donetsk £650,000 for Andrei Kanchelskis. Such was the novelty of this reverse trend that Schmeichel and Kanchelskis were two of just eleven non-British or Irish players in the final First Division campaign.

To the fans and a United board that had invested just shy of £10 million in players over three years, surely there had to be a return in terms of a title? Edwards had sanctioned the expenditure and had remained patient, but even he struggled to accept another season of anticlimax, as he explains: 'We should have actually won the League that year but we beat Leeds in both the domestic cup competitions so all they had to concentrate on was the league.

'We ended up with a huge fixture pile-up at the end of the season; so much so that I actually wrote to the League to try and extend the season, but the clubs voted against it. We had so many games to play, something like four matches in just nine days, and we just ran out of steam. And it was such a disappointment because it was all geared up to winning it and we should have won it. That's when it became that monster.'

From its inception in the boardrooms of the Big Five, Ferguson had always been an advocate of the Premier League. Unlike Brian Clough at Nottingham Forest, who had denounced the destruction of a century of tradition, Ferguson had the clarity of vision to believe the new age could only be beneficial for the likes of United. In comparison to the other twenty-one clubs, United were at least on a steady financial footing following a stock market flotation in 1991 which valued the club at £18 million and had been taken up with relish by City institutions. With that degree of backing and the guarantee of £305 million over five years from Sky's broadcasting rights deal, Ferguson sensed the potential of a seismic change at Old Trafford.

But he had to deliver.

Even the players sensed this was a tipping point for Ferguson and the club. He had come through the bleak 'Ta ra Fergie' days largely thanks to success in cup competitions, but the loss of the last Division One title to Leeds had cut deep so that even the newest recruits felt the overwhelming pressure building, as Peter Schmeichel explains: 'I had arrived in the summer of 1991 and there was a belief that Kanchelskis and I were the last bits in creating a team that could win the Championship. Then it didn't happen and it was probably the biggest disappointment of my career.

'I don't mind conceding a championship to another team if I feel they've done better than we have, but I think we were better, I always had the kind of feeling we gave them the title. In our last few games we played three of the teams that would be relegated and only took two points from them. Then we lost against Liverpool at Anfield after Leeds had beaten Sheffield United and that was it, all over. We were just finished, that was it, we just didn't have anything else. We had nothing to deliver.

'But Alex was brilliant in the dressing room after, just brilliant. Already in his mind he was building up next year, talking about how well we'd done and how close we had come and the lessons that we had learned. He believed in us, he trusted us. He told us something new was coming on the horizon, that there would be more matches on television, we would have Sunday and Monday-night games. He prepared the club, and he prepared the team for what was coming.'

Sadly, for Ferguson and United, what was coming bordered on the ignominious. They lost out to Blackburn Rovers in a bidding war for Alan Shearer when Rovers owner Jack Walker sanctioned a record-breaking £3.6 million for the Southampton striker, followed by a series of failed bids for David Hirst from Sheffield Wednesday. With the inaugural Premier League season just weeks away, Dion Dublin was recruited from Cambridge United, which, with all due respect to Dublin, barely set the pulses racing among the Old Trafford faithful, while early results on the pitch echoed a sense of frustration.

If 15 August 1992 was a historic day for the Premier League, it will go down in infamy at Old Trafford as United became the first club to concede a Premier League goal, Brian Deane's header after just five minutes going into the record books. Deane's second may not have such a place in history but it was enough to condemn United to an opening-day defeat. The mood was hardly lifted when news came through that Mark Robins, the player United had sold to help make way for Dublin's arrival, had scored twice on his Norwich City debut. Four days later, Manchester United were bottom of the Premier League, having been beaten 3–0 at home by Everton.

An eleven-game unbeaten run that included six draws may have seen United scrape into the top three for a week, but this was pedestrian fare, a pallid impression of the cavalier football being produced by the likes of Norwich and Aston Villa, both of whom were setting the kind of pace the Big Five, for whom the Premier League had ostensibly been created, could not match. Add to that Shearer scoring sixteen goals in the first half of the season for Blackburn while Dublin managed just one before breaking his leg, and the familiar frustrations with Ferguson were clear.

Yet, as so often has been the case for Ferguson, he found strength in adversity. More importantly, he found Eric Cantona.

Cantona's place in the history of the Premier League – and especially that first season – is so ingrained that he deserves (and will get) his own chapter later. The fact his arrival in the aftermath of Dublin's horrific injury had its seeds sown in dissent at Elland Road meant that Ferguson's judgement would be questioned. If Howard Wilkinson, a manager who shared Ferguson's strict disciplinary code, was willing to dispose of the Frenchman, was he really worth the risk?

For Ferguson, there was not a moment's hesitation. 'He illuminated Old Trafford. The place was in a frenzy every time he touched the ball,' the United manager would later proclaim. Paul Ince, never known to be exactly fulsome in his praise, be it for a colleague or a rival, simply said, 'He just had that aura and presence. He took responsibility away from us. It was like he said: "I'm Eric, and I'm here to win the title for you."' Less than three weeks after United's season reached its nadir with back-to-back defeats to Wimbledon and Villa, United welcomed into the fold the man who would act as the ultimate catalyst. If there is one decision that defined Ferguson's enduring strength and conviction and the dawn of the Premier League, it was that one.

There have been times when, personally, it has been difficult to like Ferguson. For a football correspondent and, later, a sports editor, his intimidation and bullying of the media and people simply trying to do their job was too much to stomach. Respect and admiration for his achievements run deep, while his generosity towards both colleagues and rivals is undoubted. Yet there could be a malice and malevolence to his methodology where the media was concerned.

In his early days at United, Ferguson was surrounded by

a group of reporters on the Manchester beat who were, by and large, his age or slightly older. People like Peter Fitton at the *Sun*, David Walker at the *Daily Mail*, the *Daily Express*'s Chief Football Writer Steve Curry and his *Express* colleague John Bean, alongside David Meek from the *Manchester Evening News*. There would be fallout and rows but generally the animus lasted no more than a week, the journalist served his penance, made something of an apology, and life moved on. Even when the calls for Ferguson's head had been loudest among United fans, there was still a loyalty towards him in the press and that fostered a reciprocal trust. If the Manchester pack were playing the long game even in the face of disbelief among United fans, it paid off.

The arrival of the Premier League changed what could be an overly reverential relationship from the media towards Ferguson. No longer could performances go under the radar as Sky's coverage dwarfed those of previous broadcast deals. It wasn't a case of the written media dictating the news agenda; now television was calling the shots, prompting a demand for inspection of every word or action.

Ferguson initially tolerated it. He still had his coterie of trusted scribes who could be relied upon. But there was a newer, hungrier breed of reporter who had not been in the trenches with Ferguson when the sack was just a defeat or so away and did not feel the same deference towards a man who, at times, seemed to take perverse pleasure in the humiliation of journalists whose words or headlines offended him. His off-the-record tirades towards journalists could be excoriating and deeply personal. And pity the journalist who stood up to Ferguson instead of taking their punishment; they could be banished into the wilderness for weeks, months and, in some cases, years.

Sky was to find that £60 million a year bought them no

immunity from Ferguson's fury. Outraged that their cameras had focused on his touchline antics at Queens Park Rangers in January 1993, where his behaviour in a 3–1 victory bordered on both the inexplicable and the lamentable as he berated the referee, his opponents and even his own players, Ferguson made it clear to executives at the broadcaster that they could expect no further cooperation for the rest of the season, albeit couched in far earthier Glaswegian tones.

Which would have been inconvenient for Sky if United had maintained their mediocre form of the early months of the campaign. Now, though, they were on a ten-match unbeaten run, with Cantona's inspiration dragging them from tenth place at the start of November to top by the time Ferguson erupted at Loftus Road.

Sky muddled through for long periods, utilising the likes of United legends Denis Law and George Best in place of Ferguson's pre- and post-match interviews. Occasionally, they would strike lucky with a word from Bryan Robson or Steve Bruce, the old guard who trusted Sky's reporters and behind-the-scenes operators who were strong enough as characters not to be afraid or worried what their manager might say. By the time it became clear United were not about to slip (they never fell below third place between Boxing Day and the last day of the season) there was a growing desperation at Sky that their triumphant arrival on the scene would be remembered mainly for the manager of the champions-elect refusing to talk to them. It was to be a familiar refrain throughout his United career, as both Sky and the BBC fell in and out of favour, depending on the United manager's whims.

Not that Ferguson or the United faithful cared. He was fixated on maintaining an astonishing run that coincided with Cantona's arrival but grew stronger in its belief with every passing victory. Aston Villa held their nerve for long periods and even Norwich were an occasional cause for concern, but there was a conviction that this was finally United's time, an unstoppable drive that reached its apotheosis on 10 April with the visit of Sheffield Wednesday to Old Trafford.

Gary Pallister takes up the story of a defining day. 'That day was massive. Wednesday were a decent side but it was a game we were expected to win. And we played quite well but we found ourselves one–nil down to a John Sheridan penalty. John's a United fan, born in Stretford round the corner from Old Trafford, and I remember Steve Bruce saying to him as he got ready to take the penalty, "Hey, you don't want to score against United really, do you?" But he didn't seem to care because he slotted it away pretty calmly. All I remember is the deathly silence around the ground, the fans knew what it meant.

'And we're missing chances. Their goalkeeper, Chris Woods, was having a great game and we're thinking this is going to be so damaging. The players felt it, the manager felt it and the fans felt it as the game was just ticking towards full time. Even if we'd managed to get a point, that was going to be damaging with Villa going so well.

'Then Brucey gets the equaliser four minutes from time, a header from Denis Irwin's corner, looping it over the top of Woodsy. Now it's going mad. There had been a problem with the referee (Mike Peck) who pulled a calf muscle or something and so they had to add on six or seven minutes of injury time for his replacement (linesman John Hilditch) to get stripped and ready to take over. I know what people say – "Oh, just play until United score" – but it took them that long to get everything sorted, it wasn't like they magicked up an extra seven minutes for no reason.

'The game had ticked into the last minute and at the time we had a tricky right-winger called Pallister! I think everybody's hearts must have sunk when, when I got the ball on the right-hand side and I tried to whip it in, sort of in front of the defender, but it's caught his head and deflected to Brucey and Brucey does what he does best in that situation, he attacks the ball really well in the box and once he gets there, he puts it away with aplomb ... and the place went nuts. I think at that moment we thought our fortunes had turned, this was the pivotal time, that was going to be the game changer and we were going to go on and win the title.

'The fans were just dumbstruck, really. They knew what it meant for us and our season. I can still see the gaffer's face – he can't believe this, wow, how have we done it? It's one of the most famous scenes in football: Brian Kidd racing on to the pitch and going down on his knees and the gaffer, well, the gaffer doesn't really know what to do. He's looking at Kiddo and can't really believe what he's seeing. That was one of the most joyous moments I had at Old Trafford.'

Five games to go and United were unstoppable. The title could be decided on the May Bank Holiday weekend, with Villa needing to beat Oldham Athletic on Sunday 2 May before United faced Blackburn at Old Trafford twenty-four hours later. Both games would be live on Sky. There was a distinct need for creativity among the broadcaster's executives and production team.

Thankfully for Sky, Bruce had struck up a friendship with it and, in particular, Geoff Shreeves who, as the match-day fixer, decided to chance his arm. He knew Bruce lived in the same close as Schmeichel and just round the corner from Paul Parker, so he asked if Sky could film them all watching the Villa game at home. Understandably wary, Bruce asked what it might entail and was told just a discreet van outside on the drive.

Sky needed the reaction. They knew the focus would be

on United whatever the Villa result and, with an hour of programming after the Super Sunday live match to fill, they would have looked foolish had there been no reference to the task – or otherwise – in front of United. Therefore, the agreement was that the footage would only be shown if Villa lost and United had won the title without kicking a ball. If the season went to the wire, then the footage would have simply been shelved. It was an inspired piece of ingenuity; Oldham went to Villa Park and won 1–0, Sky had their scenes of joy, and even Ferguson could find no reason to complain despite Bruce's leafy Cheshire close being turned into what he described as 'fucking Jodrell Bank'.

The party of three chez Bruce quickly transformed into a night of epic proportions for the United players. Bruce put the call into Ferguson, fearing the worst, only to be told 'a few quiet drinks, nothing crazy' could be tolerated. Nothing crazy quickly descended into a session of such wondrous celebration that all thoughts of Blackburn the following night were banished.

'You try and be sensible but it's difficult,' Schmeichel concedes. 'I think we needed to celebrate, we needed it to mean something in the moment. I don't think we could have waited for twenty-four hours for that celebration to flourish.

'The next day it was amazing coming into Old Trafford for the first time as champions. There's always a lot of people at the ground even three hours before when we report for a match, but this day it was full, the whole of Busby Way just packed, and it took so long to get into the reception area.'

Whether it was the hangovers, the anticlimax or a combination of both, but United started sluggishly, went a goal down and were in grave danger of letting the champagne go flat. It was then, as Schmeichel explains, the new-found mentality kicked in. 'Without anyone saying anything, I think we just all agreed within ourselves as a group that, hey, we're the champions, we can't play like this, we have to play better. From that moment on, we played our best football of the season. There was even a chance for Gary Pallister to score from a free kick, the only man who hadn't scored so far that season.

'It meant so much that Sir Matt was there to see us win the championship after his side had won the last one so long ago. For people like Sir Matt and Bobby Charlton, to see them in the aftermath of this achievement, it was just incredible.'

Looking back at the footage from such a momentous night, Ferguson appears slightly detached in his black and red club tie, suit and oversized Umbro-sponsored coat. Despite this being the cumulation of his life's work, it's as if his mind is elsewhere. There's joy, certainly, but perhaps even in that moment of history, there is no absolute satisfaction, just a recognition that this is but the first step towards glory, that there are still battles to fight, wars to win, before his appetite can be sated.

Sir Matt was the enduring face of United's magnificent past. Ferguson was its future.

3

Blue-Sky Thinking

It must have felt like betrayal. Greg Dyke, the television executive whose force of personality and vision had driven the
birth of the Premier League alongside the Big Five chairmen,
was a beaten man. He had done everything in his power, had
received support from the people he thought counted, but
lost on the single factor that would forever drive this new
institution.

Money.

Dyke's ITV had gone head-to-head with Rupert Murdoch
for the broadcasting rights to the new league – and lost to
the tune of £50 million. Understandably, it was too much for
Dyke to take. He threatened legal action over the way the
negotiations were conducted, slammed the BBC as 'Murdoch's
puppet' after the corporation took the highlights package
off ITV and raged as everything he had dreamed of building
crumbled in the face of cold, hard cash.

It is hard not to feel sympathy for Dyke, without whom the
Premier League may simply have remained a fantasy football
project. Not only had Murdoch outbid him, but he had also
been out-manoeuvred to the point where even his traditional
allies – well, at least four of them – could no longer protect
ITV. The man who had proposed a multi-million end to

television's cartel system had lost to a company even more determined to rip up the established way of operating.

The decision to abandon ITV was ultimately taken in May 1992, but the seeds of their downfall were sown by a trio of Antipodeans three years before. Murdoch provided the funds but the vision came from Sam Chisholm, a New Zealand-born television executive, and his right-hand man, Dave Hill, an Aussie with a love of all things British. Together, they took a sport described in the *Sunday Times* as 'a slum sport, played in slum stadiums and increasingly watched by slum people' and helped transform it into a league watched globally and worth well in excess of £10 billion.

Hill had joined Murdoch's global corporation in 1988 having worked for Kerry Packer's Nine Network in Australia for the previous eleven years, overseeing the formation of World Series Cricket which had revolutionised the way the sport was presented on television, bringing in coloured kits, stump mikes and on-pitch interviews, as well as making sixty of the best cricketers more money than they could ever have envisaged. In short, it was the perfect blueprint for football's own TV revolution.

Chisholm was recruited by Murdoch with the sole purpose of breathing life into the ailing body of Sky Television. In 1990 Murdoch's satellite channel was losing an estimated £2 million a week and only survived thanks to the profits from the newspaper arm of Murdoch's empire, most signif-icantly the *Sun*, which were siphoned off and pumped back into the television station. Sky was also involved in a race to the bottom with its rival, British Satellite Broadcasting, both companies haemorrhaging cash.

Within three months of Chisholm's arrival, the two com-panies merged, becoming British Sky Broadcasting (BSkyB), and while there was no likelihood of it making a profit, it gave Murdoch breathing space and, equally as important, a set of sporting rights that, while minor, allowed him a foothold in the market, as Hill explains. 'When Sky launched in February 1989, we bought the rights to Frank Bruno versus Mike Tyson, even if it was going to only half a dozen homes. But I knew the power of sport from working at Channel 9 and I'd seen the impact it had, so I said to Rupert and my fellow executives at the time that sport had to be done right. There was going to be a channel dedicated to sport and that was the birth of what was to become Sky Sports.

'We had the Bruno–Tyson fight, we had the European Snooker Masters, we became the first people to televise an England tour of the West Indies, and then I went looking to every sporting body in the UK to try and pick up rights that weren't being used – and obviously football was top of that list.'

From the merger, Sky had inherited the rights to Scottish football but also some outstanding producers and executives, most notably Andy Melvin and Vic Wakeling, whose backgrounds in the football newspaper industry at the highest level could open doors within the game and who led a young, passionate and inventive staff. Passion and invention are all very well, but as Hill quickly realised, it would need more than just those qualities if Sky was to cement its place in football.

Picking off the rights to England friendly internationals brought Hill to the attention of chairmen outside of the Big Five, those who were exploring their own avenues of opportunity while Manchester United, Arsenal, Liverpool, Everton and Spurs were being courted – and guided – by Dyke. As soon as the Premier League became enshrined in statute in the summer of 1991, Hill felt there was a door that may only have been ajar at the time but, with Murdoch and Chisholm's backing, could be barged open.

'I'd got to know Ken Bates, the Chelsea chairmen, and I loved him,' Hill explains. 'And Ken loved us because we're another buyer, and another buyer meant more money. I don't care whether you're the chairman of Barcelona or AC Milan or Scunthorpe, the one thing you need is more money.

'I started to hear more and more from Ken and then he'd bring in the Crystal Palace chairman, Ron Noades, and we'd discuss the way we thought football should be covered. At the time, it seemed like television was scared of football. If there was a live game, you'd have, say, Des Lynam come on two minutes before the match started and it was, "Okay, off we go." And there might be two minutes at the end before the programme went off air. If you wanted anything else, you had to be home on a Saturday night to watch *Match of the Day*.

'We realised Sky was seen by the chattering classes as not quite kosher and that the way we had to handle the bid was twofold. One, the money had to be right and, two, we knew were up against a wily opponent in the brilliant Greg Dyke. He is one of the great television executives of all time and I knew he wouldn't be a pushover. But we found out ITV were aiming for the top eight clubs and while I might be dreadful with numbers, I know that fourteen is going to beat eight every time, so it was pointless going to see the big clubs.'

And so began a round of discreet meetings that took Hill, Wakeling and Melvin around the country on a relentless campaign to convince as many chairmen as possible that Sky, truly, could become a force with which to be reckoned. While that argument may not have been as persuasive to those clubs who remained loyal to Dyke, it resonated with the lesser lights who believed the Premier League was going to herald a new dawn of relative equality, as Hill outlines: 'We realised at the end of the day there would have to be a vote, so if we could convince the smaller clubs that, for the first time ever in the history of English football, they were going to get a fair deal and that THEY would be put on television instead of just the elite clubs under ITV or BBC, then I thought we had a chance.

'We had to tell them we were going to treat football properly, that we would have a pre-game show, that we would develop a range of programmes during the week and that, hey, whatever you're told Sky will or will not do, we are now going to treat football with respect.'

Respectful or not, there was also the lure of the bottom line to the chairmen. Bates and Noades had been early adopters, but others saw the opportunities that, ironically, Sky's lack of viewers prompted. Their clubs would be put on air far more often, therefore they could sell shirt sponsorship at a higher level, advertising hoardings would cost more and the fact Sky was only going into a relatively small number of homes meant the only way to get your football fix was via the turnstiles. In a Taylor Report era, sell-out crowds when large sections of the ground were closed was the perfect panacea.

The triumvirate of Hill, Wakeling and Melvin was convincing and certainly felt Sky's case was receiving a fair hearing. What was needed, though, was a grand gesture – a statement of intent. It was something only Murdoch could deliver.

The Murdoch summer and Christmas parties are legendary for their cast of the most influential voices in business and politics paying fealty to 'The Boss'. Held in London's St James's, a brief and fleeting conversation with Murdoch is looked on as a golden opportunity; anything more is generally reserved for world leaders and heads of state. For Hill, December 1991 was the time to roll the ultimate dice.

He invited Bates and Noades, promising them an audience with Murdoch. The one problem was convincing Chisholm, one of the main gatekeepers to the throne, that this was a valuable use of their leader's time. Hill takes up the story. 'I wanted to introduce Ken and Ron to Rupert but Sam kind of hummed and hawed before saying he'd try and fix it up.

'So we're there at Rupert's Christmas party amongst the great and the good and we all get ushered into his office – Sam, Ken, Ron and myself – and we discuss what the Premier League is, we discuss where we're at with the minor clubs and that, basically, it would all go down to how much the rights fees would be.

'And Rupert obviously warmed to Ken and so with him and Ron pitching it and telling Rupert how they believe Sky would do the best job possible because of its marketing power, you could see Rupert getting the bit between his teeth. When Rupert gets enthusiastic about something, it's like a surge of electricity and it's, "Let's go! Yes, we can do this!" Rupert was on board; Sam was all in and we just rolled from there.'

While Murdoch's intervention allowed Bates and Noades the luxury of being able to launch their own charm offensive among their fellow chairmen, another card had fallen in Sky's favour. Before June 1991, the Big Five had been implacably unified, a single entity with an enshrined vision, courted by Dyke, able to dictate to others, safe in the knowledge their financial power was always a decisive factor.

Alan Sugar's takeover of Tottenham Hotspur in 1991 changed that dynamic. Irving Scholar had become embroiled in an ugly civil war at White Hart Lane after attempting to sell the club to Robert Maxwell, leaving the door open for Sugar to buy Scholar out after forming what was to become an ill-fated alliance with Terry Venables. While Sugar shared the vision of his erstwhile Big Five allies, he was never as aligned to the need to be wedded to Dyke and ITV. Mainly because his Amstrad company was supplying the vast majority of Sky's satellite dishes.

If Sugar's presence was any cause for concern, it did not seem to register with his Big Five colleagues, who remained singularly underwhelmed by Sky's attempts to muscle in on what they believed should be exclusively ITV and Dyke's domain. There was a loyalty which stemmed from Dyke's willingness to move the dial in their favour, as Manchester United chairman Martin Edwards explains: 'We were always grateful to Greg for showing loyalty to us because we could never break up ITV and BBC before he came along.

'And when BSkyB came along it was brand new. The question was: is it going to fail? Is it going to succeed? Financially, is it sound? Is the money guaranteed? How many people were actually going to be able to see the product? There's no point accepting a contract if it's not a success and it breaks down. People really didn't understand it fully.'

Except enough of the clubs did. Enough of the clubs realised the Premier League was a monumental change in the very fabric of English football, and that neither ITV nor the BBC felt as fundamentally committed to that change as Sky. If proof was ever needed, you only had to look back to the final day of the last Division One season and Elton Welsby cutting off Howard Wilkinson as the Leeds manager was coming to terms with his side winning the title because there was no facility at ITV to delay the adverts.

Perhaps that memory resonated on the morning of 20 May 1992 as ITV and Sky's final presentations were considered by the assembled group of twenty-two Premier League chairmen. Or perhaps it was just the potential of a financial explosion; but whatever it was, Sky were in there punching – and landing more than a few telling blows. But like everything with the formation of the League, the bidding process was mired in controversy.

A closed meeting with sealed bids; that was the order of the day. Yet with so many vested interests at play, it soon became clear the process was, in the words of Edwards, 'not quite kosher'. Hill was sat alongside Chisholm at Sky's headquarters near Heathrow Airport as the meeting unfolded. 'I felt in my heart that we had done everything we could to let the minor clubs know the way football was going to be treated, so I felt we'd have the numbers if the money was right.

'The line was open to Mr Murdoch in New York and we all knew it was going to be a scary number that was needed but we were prepared for that. Everybody had steeled themselves for the fact this was going to be over the top. Then Sam got a phone call from the meeting and he had to speak to Rupert to come up with another number. Rupert's career has been marked by these incredibly well-planned gambles where he's virtually pushed all the chips into the centre of the table.

'All I can think is that Rupert probably clenched his teeth, squared his shoulders and said, "Yeah, go ahead."'

The call from the meeting had come from Sugar, who, according to witnesses, overheard him tell Chisholm to 'blow them [ITV] out of the water'. The figure Murdoch rubber-stamped was £304 million over five years, enough to dwarf Dyke's final bid of £262 million over a similar period. Four of the Big Five remained loyal to Dyke but their power base had been eroded by the promise of a guaranteed £1.5 million a year for every club, half a million pounds more than Dyke had put on the table at the original meeting of the Big Five.

So, with around ten weeks before the start of the first Premier League season, Chisholm, Hill, Wakeling and Melvin were charged by Murdoch with providing a service that would do justice to the money he had spent. It was beyond daunting. 'I remember my first meeting with Hilly once we'd got the rights,' Melvin recalls. 'I said to him, "Dave, what's the plan?" He opened up his drawer, pulled out a piece of A4 paper and handed it to me. "That's the plan, go and make it work." And the paper was blank. I just looked at him and he said, "Yeah, that's right, the plan is whatever we want it to be."'

The decisions that would utterly transform the face of how football was covered on television were being taken by a small group of executives who did not have to adhere to a grand marketing plan or an intricately devised strategy, all they had was their instincts and expertise. What they also possessed was a conviction that British television had not grasped exactly what football means in society. Perhaps it was because Chisholm and Hill considered themselves outsiders. Perhaps because Melvin, a Scot, and Wakeling, from a northeast working-class background, had always railed against the perceived establishment mentality of the BBC and, to a lesser extent, ITV. They felt football had been given scant recognition, that the tribal passions it engendered were ignored, dismissed as the working man's ballet and left to fester in the doldrums.

Sky proudly wore its influences from American and Australian sport large, the way both countries and their television networks promoted it, treated it with respect, told the story of the players, revelled in the passion and excitement of a magnificent spectacle. All this was manna from heaven as far as David Dein was concerned.

The Arsenal vice-chairman may have stood shoulder to shoulder with Dyke and ITV in the battle for broadcast rights, but once the war had been lost, Dein welcomed Sky's approach with the zeal of a convert, as he explains. 'I'd been out to Miami to watch the Dolphins play an NFL game. Throughout the game, I was passing beers or hotdogs down the line, handing over a couple of dollars for the guy next to me to pay for his food and drink. Then I looked around and the stadium was full of families, not just men on their own. And they were all wearing some kind of Dolphins merchandise; it was mind-boggling how strongly they were buying into the event as a whole, not just the action on the field. At the time, this was completely alien to English football but there has always been a tendency to underestimate what football fans want because they'd been served up the same old fare for so long.

'Before the game, there was marching bands and cheerleaders and at half-time there was a fifteen-minute show. I couldn't even convince the Football League to extend our half-time by five minutes. At our matches, you could either go for a beer at half-time or go to the toilet, you didn't have time to do both – and if someone is bursting to go to the toilet then that's going to take precedence over another drink, so we were losing revenue as a result. It was madness; it made no sense to me. That's why I welcomed what Sky were going to do, to make things a show and spectacle.'

A marketing campaign was all well and good, but ultimately what Murdoch's money had bought was 180 minutes of live football split between Sunday afternoon and Monday evening (another nod to the NFL and their hugely successful Monday Night Football programming). With a promise to the chairmen of a channel now devoted entirely to football, the demand for more content was overwhelming. Inspiration, however, came from the most unlikely of scenarios, as Melvin recalls: 'We were very fortunate to have signed up Andy Gray when his contract as a player at Rangers was up.

'I always told my experts not to tell me what I could see with my own eyes on screen but what I couldn't see. They'd been players, they saw a bigger picture, their knowledge was precious, and Andy was the best of the lot in my opinion.

'One night we were waiting to fly back to Scotland as we

both still lived up there and were in the bar, having a few drinks. Andy was drinking Rolling Rock and I was on the San Miguels, so green bottles and brown bottles. He was explaining something to me that had happened in a game and, without thinking, lined up the green bottles one side and the brown bottles the other before moving them around as if they were players.

'I said to him, "This is brilliant, there's a programme in this." And that's how *Andy Gray's Boot Room* was born, him simply moving counters around on a board but explaining the game in a way that nobody had done before.'

Along with the *Boot Room* came *Sky Soccer Weekend*, *The Footballers' Football Show* and *Hold the Back Page*, a late-night show on Friday where football journalists dissected the week's stories. Hill knew the channel was having an impact when his assistant told him there was somebody on the phone that he had to speak to. On the line was George Best, bemoaning that one of the guests on *The Footballers' Football Show* had been talking 'shite' the week before. Hill promptly invited Best on to the next show and arguably the finest British player ever became a regular fixture.

Still, there was the small problem of persuading people to pay for the privilege of watching football on Sky. Subscription television had only been around for a few years, yet now the nation's fans were being asked to stump up for something they had historically enjoyed for free – or at least as part of their licence fee. Sky's marketing department went into overdrive. With the help of Murdoch's newspaper arm, football fans were left under no illusion that having a satellite dish on the side of your house was not just the only way to watch football, it was also something of a status symbol. The *Sun*, *News of the World* and *The Times* all ran huge promotions for cut-price subscriptions, and their pages were full of exclusive content provided by Sky. The message was unmistakable: there's a new show in town and only a Sky subscription will grant you access.

An advert was commissioned featuring one player from each of the twenty-two clubs, with Bruce Dunlop, renowned as the very pinnacle of creative talent at Sky, directing. The ninety seconds of 'A Whole New Ball Game' against the backdrop of Simple Minds' 'Alive and Kicking' still stands as a classic of its kind. 'It gave me chills the first time I saw it,' Hill admits. 'It showed we were real, that we were there, talking to the hearts of the fans. We had started to create an emotional bond between us, the broadcaster and the fans. We were taking their love, their respect, their family tradition and hopefully treating it with skill.

'We're also showing the players as personalities. In that first season of Sky's coverage, I remember Ken Bates telling me we'd changed the whole perception of Chelsea's players. Before, he said, they could walk through a Tube carriage and not be recognised because they were never seen in close-up. Now the players weren't just names, they were living, breathing personalities.'

There were missteps, of course. The Sky Strikers, a troop of dancing girls who would perform pre-match and at half-time, did not last long. Neither did the giant inflatable Sumo wrestlers that fought against each other at live games. But some innovations did stand the test of time, like actually putting the scoreline and time in the top left-hand corner despite the protests of Chisholm, who believed it was a gimmick too far.

Sky's first live game was shown on 16 August, when 'Super Sunday' was born. Teddy Sheringham followed Brian Deane into the history books, becoming the first player to score a Premier League goal live on television. The fact it was seen by a comparative handful of people meant nothing to Rupert

Murdoch; this was just the first tiny step in his vision, a moment in television history, a moment in football history probably summed up best by Hill.

'No sporting event is just an event. Whether it's curling, lawn bowls or Premier League football, sport is a microcosm of life. At any given stage, there's a gazillion stories of bravery, of tension, of cowardice, and it's up to television to bring that story out. Football is the greatest entertainment of all time so we treated it as entertainment. And I'm absolutely sure and positive that had never happened on British television before.'

A whole new ball game.

4

Money Talks

Jack Walker had money, more money than anybody had ever seen in English football.

It is one thing to have money; it is an entirely different thing to be able to spend it. And Walker wanted to spend it; he wanted his beloved Blackburn Rovers to sample the high life, to make the most of the £360 million he had made from selling his steel business. But nobody seemed to want his money.

Working on a tabloid sports desk, you hear all kinds of rumours and fantastical stories, yet when you are told by the most reliable of sources that Blackburn Rovers have made an offer to Spurs for Gary Lineker, that tests the bounds of credibility.

Blackburn Rovers of the Second Division. Tired, tatty Blackburn Rovers, attempting to sign one of English football's golden heroes, a striker whose pedigree is acclaimed throughout Europe. Why would Lineker even consider it?

I was working shifts for the *News of the World* in 1991, trying to impress in order to win a staff job, and when the Lineker to Blackburn rumour started circulating on a Friday afternoon, I was charged with getting to the bottom of it. Lineker was a friend of the paper at the time, he had been a columnist and either he or his agent was only ever a phone

call away. This time it was Lineker's agent, Jon Holmes, who
took the call.

Very patiently, he listened and, with carefully chosen
words, replied, 'Gary is very flattered at Blackburn's interest
but he will not be considering their offer,' adding, 'Completely
off the record, they can have all the money in the world but
they'll never sign who they want.'

Holmes may have been right in that moment but, in the
end, he was so, so wrong.

For all Walker's millions, for all his dreams and ambitions,
Blackburn needed more than just hard cash, they needed a
statement. The manager, Don Mackay, was a decent guy who
had twice taken Rovers to the Division Two play-offs and
missed out on both occasions, but there was no mystique to
his name, nothing that suggested he could act as the catalyst
to fulfil Walker's vision of a Lancashire powerhouse to challenge Manchester, Merseyside and London.

Yes, Mackay may have been able to sign Steve Archibald
on loan from Barcelona thanks to Walker's largesse, but
only because the striker was surplus to requirements with
Barcelona already having registered two overseas players.
Yes, Mackay may been in charge when Ossie Ardiles trotted
out for a handful of games at Ewood Park, a pit stop in the
north before returning swiftly to London. A poor start to
the 1991–92 season was enough to convince Walker and six
weeks into the campaign, Mackay was sacked.

Walker had taken full control of Rovers in January 1991
and while he remained a slightly reclusive figure, jetting in
from his Jersey home for games and staying out of the limelight, there was enough of the bombast about him to declare,
'I'm only interested in putting Rovers where they should
be. Blackburn Rovers are one of the greatest football teams
in England. They are one of the founder members [of the

Football league] and we want them right back at the top.'

Brave words about a brave future. Yet Blackburn were also a club of contradictions. Walker foresaw progress and a belief his boyhood club would be at the vanguard of the new strides that were being taken, while the chairman, Bill Fox, was also the President of the Football League and doing everything in his power to spike the guns of the proposed Premier League.

Tragically, Fox would not live long enough to witness how the battle between tradition and modernity would play out. He passed away in December 1991, but his last significant act was one that may very well have changed the course of English football. Fox may not have been able to prevent the formation of the Premier League – but he did help to convince Kenny Dalglish to become manager of Blackburn Rovers.

Dalglish – an icon at Liverpool who, as manager, had lifted three championship trophies – had resigned in February, shattered mentally and physically by the aftermath of the Hillsborough tragedy. In the wake of Mackay's sacking, rumours started to swirl that Dalglish was the target, only to be dismissed as fantasy; yet Walker was not about to allow this to become a repeat of the Lineker scenario.

'The speculation had started maybe two months before about Blackburn,' Dalglish recalls. 'There was a new owner who had a lot of money and wanted to invest it. They were talking about big names but I didn't really believe what was going on because the names they were quoting were such big names.

'The start of that season didn't go too well for them and I was asked if I would be interested in becoming the manager. I told them I needed time to check out whether it was a true story because it seemed a bit of a fantasy to me. I met with Bill Fox, who was a really nice man, then with Robert Coar, who would become chairman after Bill died, and everything seemed to check out. The wealth was real, the ambition was there, and then I met Jack.

'The biggest compliment I could pay Jack is that he didn't give the impression of a man who was that wealthy, all he wanted to do was put money back into the football club he loved and the environment he'd grown up in. He got a great enjoyment out of the club but he wanted to say thanks to the people of Blackburn and it's unbelievable what he did for the area and also the football club.

'He was very impressive; he wasn't arrogant and it just seemed to be a Cinderella story so I might as well have a go. When you've been in the position that I was as manager of Liverpool and the success we had there, there's not many places you can go that's upwards, but if you're happy and content and you've got the right people with you, you can still be successful.'

The right people included Ray Harford, recruited from Wimbledon as Dalglish's right-hand man, as well as Tony Parkes, who had been a fixture at Ewood Park and had stepped into the breach as caretaker manager in the month it took Walker, Fox and Coar to convince Dalglish to come. Results were instant, signings significant if not stellar, although they did include a record fee for a club outside the top flight when Rovers paid Everton £1.1 million for Mike Newell. It was money more than well spent when Newell scored the penalty at Wembley to beat Leicester City in the play-off final and secure Blackburn a coveted place in the Premier League. Now there would be no more sniggering at Walker's vaulting ambition. His word was as good as his money and both reverberated around the football world.

Whether Walker actually threatened to 'make Manchester United look cheap' has become lost in legend. What he did do was make Martin Edwards and Alex Ferguson 25 miles down the road look amateurish and slow when it came to laying down Blackburn's next marker, one that was arguably even more impressive than luring Dalglish back into management.

Alan Shearer had been a man in demand from the moment he scored three against Arsenal on his full debut for Southampton, a feat that surpassed the inimitable Jimmy Greaves as the youngest hat-trick scorer in England's top division. Eleven goals in thirteen England U21 appearances were followed by a goal on his full England debut, cementing his reputation as the most coveted young player in Europe. United had shown their hand towards the end of 1991, but Shearer had made it clear he would finish the season on the south coast.

If United thought their early interest would be enough to make Old Trafford an irresistible destination, they were sorely mistaken. Blackburn and Dalglish moved quickly, heeding the words of Ray Harford who had worked with Shearer at England U21s and who would wax lyrical about his qualities, both on and off the pitch. 'The best finisher you'll see, the best crosser of a ball you'll see and the kind of kid you'd be proud to have as a son-in-law,' was Harford's assessment.

A meeting was booked at the Haydock Thistle Hotel, just off junction 23 of the M6. Shearer drove north, to be met by Dalglish, Harford and Walker. Harford made the introductions, Dalglish outlined the plans, while Walker sat quietly, letting the football men do their business, knowing that if they were not able to convince Shearer of the validity of their cause, money was not about to become a deciding factor.

'All we did was tell Alan the truth, really,' explains Dalglish, 'and that this was real, not just a phase. It wouldn't be just him coming in and nobody else, we were building something that mattered. We wanted to win the title and we wanted him to be part of that.'

Those words resonated, as Shearer admits. 'I got the call from the Southampton management to say that there was interest in me from Blackburn Rovers, would I like to go and speak to them? Kenny was such an iconic figure because of what he had achieved, he'd been an unbelievable player and, of course, a success as a manager. So, I wanted to go and have a look and see what the interest was.

'The thing that struck me straight away was they actually said they want to win the Premier League. The plans were in place, there was a seriousness about them, there wasn't a single doubt in their minds that they would achieve it. Money wasn't mentioned once at that meeting, it was all about getting in the players to win the title, nothing less.

'I said I'd give them an answer before the end of the week because the talks had gone really well. I travelled back home and sat down with the wife and discussed things – and then I got a call from a representative from Manchester United who said United would like to speak to me. Of course, I said, "Well, that's really great, thank you, but I have promised I'd give Blackburn an answer before the end of the week." And that's when United said they couldn't get the money together for another couple of weeks, for whatever reason. Would I be prepared to wait?

'The fact was, I wasn't prepared to wait. I thought that if they wanted me that much, they'd put something together straight away, not make me wait, especially as I was going to give Blackburn an answer in a couple of days. I told United that, and I never heard from them again.'

In an attempt to save face, Ferguson happily told the world Shearer 'had gone for the money' and that he was 'disappointed' in that kind of attitude. Not so disappointed that he didn't, four years later, launch another bid for Shearer only to be rebuffed when Newcastle stepped forward. However, if there were any hard feelings, they were forgotten when Ferguson paid fulsome tribute at a dinner to honour Shearer's career. 'Sir Alex likes to tell people I'd have won far more in my career if I'd have signed for Manchester United,' observed Shearer on the night. 'Then again, so would he!'

Blackburn may have been sending shockwaves through the game with the record-breaking capture of Shearer – the highlight of a £12 million summer spending spree that stunned the rest of the League – but the transformation behind the scenes would have to wait a little longer. The players still rocked up at Ewood Park each morning, not knowing where they would be training, jumping in a convoy of cars as they were directed to whichever college, corporation or council pitch had been booked that day, while their own training ground was under development. It was an attitude that suited Shearer, who was never once, throughout his career, hung up on the trappings of the high life on offer.

I had become close friends with Ray Harford from my days covering Wimbledon for the local paper before I joined the *News of the World* full time. We would speak at least once a week and every conversation would either begin or end with a glowing appraisal of Shearer. One transfer that went under the radar was when Rovers paid Plymouth Argyle £500,000 for Nicky Marker, a centre half brought in mainly as defensive cover.

'It's the first day of proper training after pre-season,' Ray told me. 'All the lads are looking at Shearer, thinking is he going to give it the Billy Big Bollocks after his move, what's he like? We're playing a game and Nicky Marker launches this big punt forward, sails well over Alan's head and goes out for a goal kick. We're all waiting to see what Alan's reaction is going to be but all he does is put his thumb in the air and shouts, "All day, Nicky, I'll chase them all day."

From that moment, he was one of the lads, they accepted him straight away.'

If there was an air of humility about Shearer, he was still in for a culture shock when he dumped his training gear in the middle of the dressing room, as he had become accustomed to doing at Southampton. 'Everyone sort of looked at me, as if to say, "What are you doing?"' he recalls. 'I didn't realise that at Blackburn you had to take your own kit home and wash it.

'Having to wash your own kit was never an issue for anyone, never a problem and that's why I think we had such a good spirit because nobody got ahead of themselves. The same thing applied to the boss, and if Kenny Dalglish washed his own gear, then it was good enough for the rest of us.'

The spirit of unity was not simply confined to the dressing room and training ground at Blackburn, the whole town was galvanised by their club's new-found standing and success created by 'Uncle' Jack. His first dealings with the club had been to donate all the materials for a new stand back in 1988; now he took complete control of the redevelopment project, creating a shining white citadel which transformed the immediate landscape.

It is difficult to overestimate the impact Walker and the club had on civic pride, where almost a third of the town's population regularly filled Ewood Park. Travelling to Blackburn as a reporter in the Dalglish days was to be caught up in the fervour of the Premier League like nowhere else. While fans in Manchester, Merseyside and London took their privileged status for granted, there was an infectious exuberance about trips to Blackburn which completely counteracted accusations Walker was simply buying the League.

There was a freshness to Blackburn's football in that first season, a dedication to attack with two wide men and two strikers in harmony. Well, at least until Christmas.

Shearer was unstoppable, scoring twice on his debut against Crystal Palace and going on to score sixteen goals in just twenty-one games before tragically rupturing a cruciate ligament against Leeds United on Boxing Day. In his absence, Newell and Kevin Gallacher could not maintain the momentum and Blackburn slipped out of any reckoning, finishing fourth, thirteen points behind eventual champions, Manchester United.

The summer of 1993 brought perhaps the first signs of the new reality. A fourth-place finish had rattled the rest of the Premier League, most notably at Old Trafford where, despite their title celebrations, there was an awareness that a marker had been laid down. Alex Ferguson reacted in the only way he knew how and took up the challenge, with the first confrontation centring on Roy Keane.

Like Shearer the summer before, Keane was one of the most sought-after players in Europe. His Nottingham Forest side had been relegated in the first Premier League season and it was one of the worst kept secrets that he was leaving the City Ground. Dalglish made the first move, even shaking hands on a deal having agreed a price with Forest and wages with Keane.

Still smarting from the Shearer rejection, Ferguson mobilised his forces, as United chairman Martin Edwards explains: 'Alex was going on holiday and he said he wanted to sign Roy but had heard Blackburn were already in for him. Alex believed Roy had committed to Blackburn but that he would rather join United. The fact he was going to a direct rival obviously meant that I had to nip it in the bud.

'I remember ringing Forest and eventually agreeing a fee of £3.75 million. Of course, Roy felt a bit embarrassed because he'd given his word to Kenny Dalglish, but once he knew United were interested that was it. We were going up against somebody as wealthy as Jack Walker, we had to make a statement.'

Undeterred by Keane's volte-face, Dalglish flexed Blackburn's financial muscle elsewhere. Henning Berg had joined in January 1993 to play alongside Colin Hendry, but now Dalglish strengthened the spine of the side, handing Southampton another £2.4 million to bring in goalkeeper Tim Flowers. David Batty was recruited to fill the Keane-shaped hole in midfield, albeit for £1 million less than Keane would have cost, while Graeme Le Saux moved from Chelsea. With Shearer fit again and thriving on the service of Jason Wilcox and Stuart Ripley from the flanks, this was a team with which to be reckoned.

For Le Saux, it was a leap of faith but one that he never regretted, as he explains: 'I did a lot of research when I heard Blackburn were interested in me and I thought, "This could be incredible." But I didn't even know where Blackburn was. I knew it was in the north but I didn't know how far north of Manchester it was, was it further west than Preston?

'I started looking where I could fit in and thinking about working with Kenny Dalglish, who was one of my heroes. Straight away I sensed there was a common goal within the hierarchy, an identity I spotted immediately. From the first meeting with Kenny and Ray Harford to the first training session, we were all working together for the same goal that hadn't existed at Chelsea.

'You're thrown into it, and you're emotionally involved, and it felt like a very galvanised group: highly competitive based on the highest work ethic, attention to detail and process. All those things were fuel to me; it was warm, friendly, happy, positive and ambitious. Nobody was any better than anybody else, just a real sense of identity.

'Jack Walker set that culture. He was very down to earth;

he would love mixing with the players and would speak to us before a game but never interfere. If he'd been aloof and grand, I suspect it would have been more difficult for us to have that identity, to reinforce that culture. A little example would be when he'd phone my dad up, who also lived in Jersey, and say, "I've got a spare seat on my plane to go over for the match, do you fancy coming?" And my dad wasn't in awe of going on a private jet, it was the fact Jack had bothered to even think of him.'

For all the off-the-field qualities Blackburn possessed, nothing they could do on the pitch could combat United's dominance. Ferguson's side went top on 23 August and never slipped from that for the rest of the season, at one stage opening a sixteen-point gap over Rovers and cantering to the title, eight points clear of Dalglish's side – and all this despite Shearer's thirty-one goals.

Though the season had been a procession, Blackburn did enough to give Ferguson pause for thought when they took four points off the champions over the two games, even if there was little solace in the final table.

Going head-to-head with United meant facing Ferguson down once more in the transfer market and this time the battleground was Norwich City's Chris Sutton, with Arsenal in the mix to shake things up and add a little more spice. The bidding war was ferocious, with Blackburn barely blinking at the prospect of laying out £5 million. For once the market was too rich for United and although Arsenal put up a fight, again the prospect of playing for Dalglish was enough to convince Sutton to head north. It was a triumph for Walker and sent the strongest message yet that everything Dalglish had laid before Shearer two years earlier was more than just empty promises.

I remember travelling north in the summer of 1994 to

interview a player at Liverpool for a pre-season piece. Before heading back to London, I called in on Ray Harford and, as would invariably be the case, we ended up having dinner at his favourite restaurant. Normally deadpan and archly cynical, there was something unusually excitable about Ray that night.

'It's the players,' he insisted. 'I can see something in their eyes, something that wasn't there last season or the season before. They really believe they can win the League this season. I've been waiting to see that; I don't think anyone can stop us.'

Now Ray would never claim to be a prophet, but seven matches unbeaten at the start of the season with Shearer and Sutton – or as we in the tabloids insisted, SAS – matching each other goal for goal with six apiece, underlined the belief flooding through every Blackburn player. But the fixture against Manchester United loomed large at the end of October.

It would end in a controversial victory for the champions, Blackburn having had Henning Berg sent off erroneously, but a 4–2 scoreline did nothing to dent the confidence coursing through Dalglish's side, as Le Saux explains: 'This would be a vital game for our development. I don't remember being upset with the result of the game because we took so many positives out of it.

'Even with ten men we took the game to them, we weren't going to give up, we hadn't changed our way of play. We didn't stop, we never let them have an easy moment in the game, we were competitive throughout the whole game. The atmosphere was incredible and that's a part of it because the fans believed that we could beat Manchester United, and we were the real deal.'

Fortified by the performance against United, if not the result, Blackburn emerged an unstoppable force. Ten wins from their next eleven matches, the historically tough Christmas period treated like a mid-summer trot, it was the kind of run that breeds its own momentum, as Chris Sutton explains: 'The run we went on after United was probably out of anger as much as anything, the fact that we felt wronged, so in many respects we can look back and say that that did us a favour.

'I remember going into games, especially before Christmas, and just knowing we were going to win – and you shouldn't really feel like that as a player, but we were so confident in the way we were playing that we'd analyse the opposition and think, "We're just going to beat you up and outplay you and outwork you."'

Le Saux agrees. 'You try and describe what you mean by momentum and it's the fact we were looking forward to every game, we were in our groove, training was really established, and I think every one of us was at our peak and playing at our highest level – then matches become self-fulfilling prophecies. It doesn't mean you can't lose a game, but you feel you have that protection around you.'

Inevitably the run did come to an end – and at Old Trafford to boot – on 22 January, with a 1–0 defeat courtesy of Eric Cantona's eightieth-minute winner. It was to be the last impact the Frenchman had on the title race as three days later he launched himself into the Selhurst Park crowd feet first and was banned for the rest of the season. If the football gods were smiling on Dalglish and his team, there was still plenty of work to do.

'You can talk about Cantona's suspension, you can find all these reasons, but the best team wins the league,' he insists. 'Of course, him being missed didn't help them but we didn't think about that, we thought about ourselves and what we had to do. You don't start working out permutations. I never sat down and thought, "There's four games coming up, we need twelve points out of this, or we could get six." I never did that because it would only be my predictions and you don't win football matches with predictions, you win them with facts.'

Despite all Dalglish's pragmatism, Blackburn were stumbling in the closing stages of the season and only the points they had garnered from the amazing winter run sustained their position at the top of the table as United, even without the totemic Cantona, put a run of eight straight wins together going into the last day of the season.

Shearer's winner against Newcastle meant Blackburn had a two-point lead going into the final game, away at Liverpool, while United went to West Ham. A win would give Blackburn the title, anything less and their destiny was out of their hands. Even for the unflappable Dalglish, pressure was telling on both him and the players. 'Aye, we were just anxious to get it over the line because it was a long journey for them. To get that close and not see it through would have been difficult.

'I don't think they were actually afraid of winning but some of them might be thinking, "We're never going to get this close again, never going to win a championship or a medal."'

What transpired at Anfield and Upton Park provided one of the most dramatic days the Premier League has seen – not just in its infancy but throughout the thirty years of its history.

Shearer gave Blackburn the lead against Liverpool, his celebration muted – he knew there was still too long a journey to endure. The mood among the travelling Blackburn fans edged towards ecstasy when the news filtered through from east London that Michael Hughes had given West Ham the lead.

Surely nothing now could derail their dream?

Suddenly Brian McClair equalised for United. And worse, Liverpool were intent on spoiling the party as goals from John

Barnes and Jamie Redknapp meant United were just a point behind and with around forty minutes to find a winner at West Ham. If there is an equivalent of purgatory in football, Blackburn had found themselves there.

For once, Shearer and Sutton came up short, missing big chances to put the game beyond reach, and then it's just a clock ticking down. Sky's match-day staff took a decision not to keep Dalglish informed of events at West Ham; they wanted the drama etched on his face. Only the Blackburn fans via transistor radios were keeping their manager abreast of the situation. With minutes still remaining at Anfield, Dalglish suddenly gets pulled back into the throng behind his dugout, he emerges, turns to question – and then a beam of delight lights his face.

The game still had ninety seconds to run but Blackburn players were overcome by their achievement. Tim Sherwood, with his fists clenched in celebration, eyes closed, ecstatic; Tim Flowers, running around his penalty area, arms outstretched, Colin Hendry appearing to offer a prayer of thanks. Even Harford, the least demonstrative of men, engulfed Dalglish in a bear hug on the sidelines, all thoughts of professional demeanour to the end forgotten.

For Shearer, it was almost too much to bear. 'For five or ten seconds, I thought we'd lost it, that United had won. But then all of a sudden, we could see Blackburn fans going mad behind the goal. Then I could see Kenny and Ray hugging on the touchline and Jack Walker coming down, crying. They'd told me when I met them that first day that we would win the Premier League – and to do it within three years was unbelievable.'

Within a year, though, the dream was over. Dalglish resigned and took a boardroom position, convinced he had nothing more to offer as a manager. Harford took the reins but made the fatal mistake of not reinforcing the Blackburn squad from a position of strength and the squad, exhausted from the previous campaign, struggled to rediscover anything like the form that had taken them to the title. They finished seventh, twenty-one points behind champions United. Shearer still struck with astonishing regularity, but his thirty-one goals would be the last he scored for Blackburn.

There was a new and exciting show in town, United's Class of '92 had graduated with stunning results; Newcastle were now everybody's darlings as Kevin Keegan conjured up fantasy and fun on Tyneside, while Liverpool and Arsenal had overtaken Blackburn, barely breaking stride. Four years later, Blackburn were relegated in the same season as United won the Treble.

The Premier League had bitten back. It was as if an asterisk had been placed alongside Blackburn's name in the record books with the footnote insisting the traditional powers would never allow themselves to be usurped by an upstart again.

5

Born Is the King

As with everything concerning Eric Cantona, there are always myriad interpretations. Ask him to describe himself on the football pitch, and the word he uses is *fauve*.

The literal translation from French is 'wildcat'; and Cantona obviously sees in himself that sense of feline grace, elan and alertness. Yet dig a little deeper and *fauve* describes a style of painting that flourished in France at the turn of the twentieth century, epitomised by pure, brilliant colour aggressively applied straight from the paint tubes to create a sense of explosion on the canvas.

His words and actions have probably been scrutinised, analysed and dissected more than any player's in Premier League history. His cultural impact on the English game may, at times, have been overstated, as we in the media sought to discover an ideology in the upturned collar and ramrod-straight back, but without him there is no foreign line of succession: no Klinsmann, no Bergkamp, no Zola, no Henry, no Ronaldo.

Without Cantona, who would have fulfilled the role of Sky's first charismatic hero? Shearer? Keane? It's difficult to envisage either of them daubing those early years of the Premier League with the same vivid palette, no matter how majestic their feats.

And what of Manchester United? Has there been a single figure in a red shirt who personified everything demanded of them by Alex Ferguson; that combination of coruscating attacking brilliance, intelligence and swagger that transformed Old Trafford and rekindled memories of Best, Law and Charlton that had long faded amid twenty-six years of mediocrity?

Football as art. Football as wild imagination. Football as an escape from the drudgery of a binary thought process. Football as life as it should be lived. For Cantona, that was the very essence of his existence. And when that passion was gone, so was he.

The mark he made on the English game is indelible, yet the one the Premier League made on Cantona is equally strong. 'I came from France where they wanted us to be all the same, you know, like thousands of sheep on the land. I am not talking about the colour of people's skin but if you are the one black sheep, somebody who is different, they don't give you a chance to express yourself, they want to manipulate you.

'I never wanted to be manipulated, I always needed to express myself and for me in England, I was able to do this with my feeling and my instinct – and they accepted me. I think it's odd that the people we love are different.

'If we love Jim Morrison, it's because he was different. If we love Kurt Cobain, it's because he was different. The same with Amy Winehouse, Jimi Hendrix or Arthur Rimbaud or Marlon Brando, all have that certain kind of personality. It's what I searched my whole life for before I arrived in England and in England, the people helped me express myself.'

Self-expression and a premature demise (at least in terms of his football career); it is easy to see why Cantona aligns himself with the likes of Cobain, Hendrix and Rimbaud. There was always something of the tortured artist about Cantona that his arrogance could never wholly disguise, as if he was searching for something far more important than the prosaic nature of three points or even a piece of silverware, something that stirred his soul, as he explains: 'I just play football for enjoyment, always for the beauty of the game.

'Of course, I was a winner; I wanted to win but always in a good way. You can feel the players who kept this spontaneity and love of the game. I love to have a certain relationship with the ball, I love when I feel comfortable in the shirt, in the kit, everything. If I don't feel comfortable, I cannot play my game.

'I didn't know a lot about English football before I arrived because in my time, we didn't have a lot of games on TV, but what I had was that everybody wanted to play the game to win. In other countries, they play to not lose. You have a lot of passion in Spain or Italy or Germany, but England was special, and it was more than football, it was like the players were rock stars, you know.

'England is special in football, it's special in music, it's special in a lot of things. And they could accept somebody who is a certain kind of personality, somebody who is a bit different but can be accepted and loved also.'

Cantona's acceptance at Old Trafford was instant. At the time of his arrival, Darren Ferguson was still part of the United squad and, inevitably, was referred to in the dressing room as 'Son Of', yet even Ferguson junior joked his father would not have minded if he had moved out of the family home if it meant making room for Cantona.

Alex Ferguson's adoration of the Frenchman was complete, as teammate Paul Parker explains: 'You could see the Boss just idolised him. Eric could get away with more than the rest of us but not to the point where there was ever going to be a mutiny, it was just the way of managing him, to get the best out of him, to make Eric feel comfortable – and he'd never been at a club where he felt comfortable.

'There was the appreciation and respect for him as a footballer but also as a person. Sir Alex would sometimes come down to the dressing room and if he saw the door open, he'd come in. When he did, there was a collective intake of breath from the players because you normally knew all the air was about to be sucked out of the room.

'But the Boss would have a big smile on his face if he saw Eric there and he'd go sit there next to him and they'd start speaking in this new language, Glaswegian-French we called it, and it was a bit excruciating but then you'd see everybody's shoulders come forward; we relaxed because you know nobody's getting pinned to the wall.'

The brilliance of Ferguson's man-management of Cantona was to make him believe he was operating outside of authority when, in fact, the United manager still had total control of his maverick ... well, up to a point.

The Frenchman's constant determination to rail against those who would 'manipulate' him was the stuff of infamy in his homeland. A three-match ban for a horrifically high tackle on an opponent while at Auxerre, a year's suspension from international football after calling France manager Henri Michel a 'sack of shit' live on television, a one-month ban by Marseille after he kicked the ball into a crowd and ripped off his shirt after being substituted. Cantona's rap sheet was an extensive one. Perceived injustice was met by petulance and vitriol, most notably when, at Nimes, he faced a French Football Federation disciplinary panel for throwing the ball at the referee.

Handed an initial one-month ban, that was increased to two when he insulted each of the panel as 'idiots'; Cantona subsequently announced his 'retirement' on 16 December

1991, only for Michel Platini to convince him to reconsider. Six weeks later, Cantona signed for Leeds.

But if French football and its culture were stifling, life at Elland Road was far from liberating. Howard Wilkinson tolerated Cantona but never fully trusted him, seemingly itching to find a reason not to select him despite the nine goals in twenty-eight games, many of which had helped Leeds to the last ever First Division title. For a man who appreciated the finer things in life when it came to wine and cigars, Wilkinson had no time for luxury in the form of Cantona.

Whether the two managers, who remain good friends to this day, ever spoke about the travails of life with Cantona remains unknown, but when Ferguson received a phone call from his chairman, Martin Edwards, to say there was a chance to snatch Cantona away from the champions, Ferguson's reaction was one of unconfined enthusiasm. Having failed to sign either Alan Shearer or David Hirst and then losing Dion Dublin to a broken leg, Ferguson knew this was a signing *in extremis*. It was, however, to be the defining decision of his career.

For Cantona, there was the realisation that this, finally, was the place he could make indelibly his own. 'I dreamed about the passing football; pass, move, pass, move, this was what Manchester United were about, they matched my dream. I see football as an art because you create something. You represent all the movements of the players on the pitch and if you drew it, then you'd make a wonderful piece of art. And that was the way Manchester United liked to play.

'It was the beginning of a revolution so when you arrive at a club like this, you have to prove everything because people expect something. I have something to prove but do I have to do or say something to satisfy everybody? Yes, but in my own way. I have to express myself for the team and the club – and

Alex Ferguson was the perfect manager for that, he helped everybody express themselves as personalities.

'He wasn't afraid to be in front of personalities. Some managers take players who are easy to manage, easy to control, but what is great about Alex Ferguson is he had strong personalities – Schmeichel, Robson, Keane – and he could deal with them, and more than that he helped them express themselves to be part of the team but he was still stronger than anyone.'

Cantona, even at his most lyrical, struggles to define the relationship he had with Ferguson. At times, it was paternal, at others, more ingrained, as the Frenchman tries to explain: 'I don't know what he has, a great psychology, I suppose. A great manager, a great psychologist, yes, but it was also like love.

'I knew with him that I could express myself and I didn't want to know more. I don't want to know why I love my wife, love is not intellectual, it's instinctual, you just feel those things and when you start to understand too many things, you lose everything.

'Sometimes, you ask yourself, "Why does a fan love me?" and I don't want to know why they love me because if I start to understand why maybe I will give them what they expect. But maybe they love me for my instinctive behaviour and that's why life is so wonderful and it's better not to analyse everything.'

Cantona's impact on the pitch was immediate as the infant Premier League fell in thrall to his brilliance. If United had slumbered behind the likes of Blackburn, Aston Villa and Norwich City in the first half of the season, Cantona galvanised a goal-shy side and allowed Ferguson to make a tactical tweak of playing him alongside Mark Hughes and dropping Brian McClair back into midfield. United did not look back, losing just two games after the Frenchman's arrival, and Cantona's nine goals in twenty-one games plus a host of assists saw them claim the first title of the Premier League era.

Continued dominance seemed assured when United made it successive titles a year later, with Cantona's twenty-six goals earning him the Professional Footballers' Association Player of the Year crown. But the warning signs were already there. In his first season at Old Trafford, Cantona had been fined £1,000 for spitting at a Leeds fan on his first return to Elland Road, while back-to-back red cards against Swindon Town and Arsenal had seen him banned for five matches. It was never enough to derail United's Premier League ambitions – or their FA Cup hopes, where his two penalties in the final versus Chelsea helped earn United a historic Double.

Ferguson instinctively sensed there was something building within his talisman. In training, players were on their guard whenever Cantona gave a pass that fell even minutely below his impeccable standards because his next instinct was to win the ball back, no matter what the cost to the health of those around him. In matches, he was ordered by Ferguson not to tackle, to simply wait for teammates to pass him the ball, not to try to win it back himself.

Perhaps the off-field pressures played their own part. Gary Pallister recalls being out for a night with Cantona, and the striker being spat on from the mezzanine level by rival fans intent on goading a reaction, which he denied them. Selhurst Park was to be the setting for the nadir of Cantona's relationship with English football. To those of us covering many of United's matches at the time, it felt like an inevitability, such was the line he constantly trod.

The circumstances and aftermath of that astonishing evening in January 1995 have been only too well documented and need no repetition here. I was at the game, covering it for the *News of the World*, albeit not 'live' as it was a midweek match. To be honest, all I saw was a figure in a black bomber jacket descending from close to the back of the stand to pitch-side and then Cantona caught in a maelstrom of limbs. To this day, only Zinedine Zidane's World Cup final headbutt on Marco Materazzi and subsequent red card comes close to the shock of what unfolded.

Frankly, Cantona's sense of contrition is towards his team-mates and United, rather than for his actions on the night. In fact, there's an almost perverse pleasure in what happened when he says, 'I remember the feeling in the dressing room, it was something special. It's an experience and a wonderful experience, it's great to have a situation like this, you know, to learn a lot of things. Learn about yourself, learn about others.

'I'm a kind of man who wants to live more, as much experience as possible. I want to put myself in a certain kind of situation, to live the experience. It was exciting to me, it was that or drugs. I prefer to play football in front of thousands of people, it gives me adrenalin; I prefer to go onstage in the theatre, or on the set of a movie. I prefer to create a certain kind of relationship with the people around me, to feel alive.

'I think when a player is missing, you can play one game without that player. If you play one or two games without them, you can handle the situation. But after, if you don't play with one of these players who make the team for a few weeks, I think it can make the difference.

'And I think we didn't win it [the title] because we were used to playing all together and one piece was missing. If it was Schmeichel or Irwin or Paul Ince or Roy Keane, it would have been exactly the same, I think. It's why we lost it, so it was my fault. I don't regret the thing I did, I feel guilty because we didn't win the League.'

It's difficult to believe, in an age of social media and instant analysis and opinions, that Cantona could possibly have survived in English football. In 1995, Ferguson seethed that it made *News at 10* and that Sky played it once or twice AN HOUR for the following few days. But there was no intervention or headline-hogging denunciations from politicians, no Twitter polls or memes; nothing except a gnawing fear from within Old Trafford that a life ban was a possibility.

For Cantona, it was liberation. 'I felt free. [The media] could spend months in front of my house. I felt free, free to stay in, go out, free to do whatever I wanted. Even if I went out naked, I didn't care. They do their job, I do mine. I have nothing to hide.

'It wasn't hard but what was hard was to not play football, to play the games. I trained hard, even more than before, but I wasn't allowed the opportunity to play even a friendly game. That was hard, but the other things? I didn't care.

'I learned a lot about the fans, the people at the club, my teammates. Sometimes we speak about families, you know, the club is a family or something – and in most clubs it's not like this but my experience in this moment shows exactly that Manchester United is a family.

'The club (could have) sacked me, the fans could have been disappointed and hated me, my teammates also. I think in many clubs, I would maybe have been sacked but Manchester United offered me two more years of a contract. I was allowed to leave if I wanted to leave; they always said that to me, "If you want to leave, you can leave." And if you say that to me, I stay. If you don't allow me to leave, I will leave!'

The offer to allow Cantona to leave came from Ferguson, who had flown to Paris for what was inevitably billed a summit meeting. In truth, Ferguson feared the worst after his star had been penalised for playing a behind-closed-doors friendly, a club mistake but one that impacted Cantona more forcefully than even the threat of prison. The feat of changing Cantona's mind was one of the great diplomatic coups of Ferguson's time at Old Trafford.

His reward was a rejuvenated Cantona who marked his comeback with a penalty against Liverpool on 1 October 1995, and a goal almost every other game for the remainder of the campaign, as United held off Newcastle to land their third title in four years, the most significant being the winner at St James' to break every Geordie's heart.

Just to show there were no lasting recriminations towards Cantona from the press, he was voted the Football Writers' Association Footballer of the Year. I was part of the FWA's National Committee at the time and was on hand to witness his entrance into the VIP reception. Obviously, nobody at United had briefed him on the dress code because he arrived in a bow tie and dinner jacket for a less formal lounge-suit event. Unfazed, he simply took off his dicky bow, undid two buttons on his dress shirt and immediately became the coolest man in a room of six hundred people. Two days later, he scored the only goal in the FA Cup final to beat Liverpool and complete another Double for United.

The ending, a year later, after yet another title triumph for United, should have been straightforward to predict. Cantona scored just fifteen goals in fifty appearances despite United's dominance in the League, and the responsibility of captaincy, gifted to him by Ferguson at the start of the season, perhaps quelled some of the fire. Certainly, this was a far tamer Cantona.

As is ever the case, word of Cantona's impending exit had reached the press. One of Ferguson's closest media confidants, Bob Cass of the *Mail on Sunday*, had been given a tip that retirement was imminent and approached Ferguson for a steer, if not absolute confirmation. To many of us who knew

Bob and his brilliance as a story-getter, what Ferguson did still sticks in the craw: an outright denial saw Bob ignore the story, only for it to break the following day, well after the *Mail on Sunday* had gone to press. It is not too far of a leap to suggest that could have cost Bob his job although, thankfully, he had more loyal employers than contacts.

For Cantona, the realisation that the spirit was gone came well before the actual announcement of his retirement. 'I'm afraid about one thing – the emptiness. I hate emptiness. When I lost the passion, lost the fire in me, I just retired. I tried to find some wood somewhere to light it again, but I knew it was the end.

'I admire the players who play until the age of forty but . . .'

He deserved to go out on his own terms. This was a man who revolutionised the English game with his dedication to training, his demands for perfection, the standards he set on the pitch that helped guide Manchester United to so much success in the short time he illuminated Old Trafford.

Yes, his arrogance could be monstrous, his behaviour beyond the pale at times, whether it was extracting his own sense of justice against a fan or an opponent who had disrespected him, but even his most infamous incident at Selhurst Park prompted a debate about xenophobia and racism in our game that had rarely been aired so freely. He destroyed the image of the foreign player as somehow effete in nature, who could not cope with the demands of the yeoman's game. Cope? He damn well thrived, his genius forever unshackled.

If his pronouncements sometimes bordered on the overly theatrical and pompous, then surely he can be forgiven because of what he gave us on the pitch. The soul of a poet shod in Nike boots; the way he describes the game reminds you of just why he dazzled.

'You have to anticipate, you have to anticipate a lot of

movements from your opponents, from your teammates. Sometimes you have eighty thousand people in the stand, and you give the ball to somebody, and it surprises everybody. So, it's what I like in football, the way you play it and the beauty of the game.

'It's like the lions or the tigers or, you know, the panthers, the way they move. Like they are sleeping but if they move quickly, they move quickly. They are not sleeping, no, they rise and are alert and the way they run is so elegant. In French, we call them *fauve*, the perfect way to run, to think, to behave.

'And also, what football represents in society. When we are young, it's a way to escape poverty, it's a way to have a certain kind of education. Football and music are very important for some working-class people to have another chance to succeed. You can play football anywhere, even in your living room, with two or three pairs of socks, and you make a goal.

'Like we did when we were young.'

6

Dying of the Light

The Premier League came fifteen years too late for Brian Clough. In his prime, he had the man-management prowess of Ferguson, the swagger of Mourinho and the charisma of Klopp. While he may not have had the humility of Pep Guardiola, he had a system of play which would have had the Spaniard drooling.

Yet the Clough that welcomed the dawn of the Premier League was a broken shell of the man who had dominated English football with both Derby County and Nottingham Forest. And 'welcomed' would be a stretch, given Clough's regular diatribes against change, modernity and the encroachment of those forces many regarded as progressive but which Clough sensed as destructive.

As part of a generation of reporters taking their first steps in the industry, the latter years of Clough were instructive only in as much as I had never encountered such rudeness and contempt for journalists. Add to that the allegations of corruption that swirled around him even before they were made public in the High Court in 1993, and there was a feeling the Premier League was better off without him.

But now, all these years later, researching this book made me realise just why so many of my older colleagues at the time spoke of Clough in such reverential terms, why his foibles were tolerated and why, whether he was a product of simpler times, there can be no doubting his genius as a football manager.

At his peak, there was a courage to Clough. Courage in the way his teams played the game. Courage in the way he stood by his principles. Courage in the way he constantly stood up to authority even when it most likely cost him the chance to manage his country. He stood steadfast in what he believed and never willingly took a backwards step.

Yet in all those qualities lies the seeds of his demise. At fifty-seven, he was not an old man when the Premier League was launched, not by the standards of Sir Alex Ferguson, Sir Bobby Robson and Roy Hodgson, who were – and in some cases still are – managing at the highest level in their seventies. But while the likes of Ferguson, Robson and Hodgson possessed the unerring ability to adapt and take on new ideas, Clough refused to change.

'I can't compromise to save my life,' he told Sky Sport's Nick Collins in the final days of his Forest career, just weeks before his retirement was announced and their relegation from the Premier League in that first season was confirmed – and that was the root of his demise.

For the first time since 1974 and his controversial departure from Leeds United after just seven chaotic weeks, Clough was no longer in charge of his own destiny. He was powerless to prevent Forest's ignominious slide down the table and his sharpness of mind had been dulled by a combination of alcohol and fatigue.

Pat Murphy, in his excellent biography of Clough, *His Way*, chronicles that final season in a chapter entitled 'Annus Horribilis'. The overriding sentiment is of a man out of his time, raging against the dying of the light, but without the power and fury he once possessed to keep the darkness at bay.

That first Premier League season, Forest were the softest of touches. They may have been the first side to win a game live on Sky, beating Liverpool thanks to that Teddy Sheringham goal, but it was to be the striker's last meaningful act for Forest. And the impact of his £2.1 million move to Spurs would have huge ramifications for Clough – both on and off the pitch.

Without Sheringham, who went on to score twenty-eight times for Spurs that season, Forest were bereft in front of goal. His departure would also lead to Clough's name being dragged through the High Court when the Tottenham chairman, Alan Sugar, claimed he had been told by his manager, Terry Venables, that Clough 'liked a bung' and that he had been paid a £50,000 sweetener to incentivise Sheringham's move.

'Alan Sugar is a spiv and a barrow boy,' was Clough's retort, but the fact that Sugar's allegations were met by hardly a raised eyebrow among managers, chairmen and the media alike told its own story. Earlier that year, I had sat with a former Forest executive who detailed how increasingly large sums would disappear from transfers and how those payment instructions would often be at the behest of Clough himself.

There was not a strong enough paper trail to convince lawyers at the *News of the World*, but a three-man Premier League panel had no such reservations and, after an inquiry, found that, 'On the balance of evidence, we felt he [Clough] was guilty of taking bungs. The evidence was pretty strong.' Perhaps in deference to Clough's reputation combined with his ill-health, the Premier League decided against a disciplinary charge.

The damage to his reputation, though, was cumulative. The evidence of Forest's downfall was plain for everybody to see as Clough, once so astute and courageous in the transfer market,

failed, in the space of four months, to replace Sheringham
or defenders Des Walker and Darren Wassell, despite raking
in £5 million from their exits. Clough's refusal to pay either
inflated fees or salaries was at odds with the demands of
the new age, where spending money to stay among the elite,
attracting further riches, seemed smart business practice.

By common consent, Stan Collymore's arrival would have
certainly aided the fight against relegation, yet Clough refused
to pay Southend an extra £250,000 to take the fee to £2 million, thereby scuppering the move. Clough's principles may
have remained intact, but his reputation was beginning to
fracture, especially when you consider Forest paid Southend
an initial £2.25 million two months after Clough's retirement
and the striker's goals led the club back to the top flight at the
first time of asking.

If his transfer dealings were flawed, Clough's treatment of
players was idiosyncratic, to say the least, and bordered on
bizarre at times. Several former Forest players have peppered
their memoirs with tales of Clough's unorthodox methods,
like the time he took the players to an Amsterdam brothel
ahead of a European Cup clash with Ajax (they won). Or the
time the squad drank champagne into the early hours the
night before the League Cup final against Wolves (they lost).

Yet those were the days when Clough could comfortably
point to two League titles and two European Cups in order to
assuage any criticism of his methodology. His word was law
at the City Ground and no mind was given to the changing
times when players could not simply be insulted, bullied or
even physically intimidated. Some, like Roy Keane, tolerated
Clough's excesses and accepted being punched when the manager felt his young star needed to be brought into line.

Twice Keane was struck: once when he gave away a goal
against Crystal Palace in the FA Cup after under-hitting a

back pass and once when he and several teammates broke curfew on a training trip to Jersey. Recalling the Palace incident, Keane said in a later interview, 'Brian Clough was a genius. Did I take it badly? No. He was upset, he was heated and he punched me. I came in the next day and trained because my loyalty is always towards Brian Clough because of the fact he signed me, gave me my debut and I will always be grateful for that.'

Keane, however, was fast becoming an exception. Gary McAllister, a shrewd judge of character, refused to sign for Forest from Leicester City after Clough's horrific timekeeping, combined with what McAllister considered to be pointedly intrusive questions about his marital status and personal life. Instead he chose Leeds, helping Howard Wilkinson's side to the title two years later. It was a needless mistake on Clough's part.

His treatment of Wassell was even more outlandish. The pair clashed in a reserve team game after the defender injured his hand in the first half. Seeking treatment, Wassell was disgusted when Clough grabbed his hand, spat on it, rubbed in the saliva and simply expected the player to get on with the second half. The relationship, which was already shaky, deteriorated to the point of collapse and Wassell left for Forest's bitter rivals, Derby County.

While Clough in his prime ruled through a combination of fear, respect and the quickest of wits, his latter years were marked by an almost perverse desire to humiliate. The attempts at humour were too often cruel, as his captain, Stuart Pearce, recalls. 'We signed a fella called David Currie from Barnsley for £650,000 one summer and we were about three weeks into pre-season.

'Dave had only been at the club for about three weeks and we went to play Derby in a friendly. We were sat in the

Baseball Ground and when Cloughie was in the dressing room, no one said a word. So, all the players were sat around about ten minutes before we were going out to play.

'And he [Clough] looked across the dressing room to Dave Currie, stared him straight in the eyes and said, "Have you found yourself a house yet, Dave?"

'Dave said, "No, not yet, Boss."

'"Don't bother, son," Cloughie went. After three weeks at the club, he'd decided, "He ain't for me."' Currie made only eight appearances for Forest before he was sold.

A football dressing room can be a forgiving place. If managers behave in a way that would see them disciplined in any other business but are still winning games, players will turn a blind eye, accepting it as part of the price of success. But an irrational manager who has lost the winning habit becomes either a figure of fun or a festering presence. Clough became the latter in his last season.

His decision-making was, at times, absurd. Even his most loyal lieutenants were astonished that Clough refused to work on set pieces, a factor of the game that was becoming more important with every season. His training methods were solely tailored to a passing game which, while admirable in some respects, was still an abdication of responsibility when more limited teams like Wimbledon and Sheffield United were hugely competitive in the new league because of their organisation and tactical understanding.

Yet still Clough persisted with a style of play and man-management that was virtually obsolete. Forest's pre-match routine was carved in stone: a week of six-a-sides was followed on match day by Clough placing a ball on a table and say, 'This is the tool you work with – treat it kindly and you'll be okay. If you whack it over the stand, that's not our style. Get hold of it and caress it.' Then he would insist on the players sitting with their legs stretched out and smile because his belief was a relaxed player did himself justice. So when opponents were working on tactics and game-plans, organisation and understanding, Forest were preparing for a day on the beach.

Certainly, Clough deserves all the plaudits for what he achieved over the years at Forest, but smart, forward-thinking managers like Ferguson and Kenny Dalglish recognised the world of the Premier League was the fastest changing landscape in sport; players simply would not tolerate being treated like chattels, they demanded respect and they demanded to learn and improve.

Ferguson's treatment of Eric Cantona would have been anathema to Clough. In Clough's book, you did not make allowances for different personalities, they made allowances for your own maverick ways. As power shifted subtly towards the players, Clough was an anachronism, a manager completely out of time and place.

His decision-making was becoming increasingly warped, playing his two best players, Keane and his own son Nigel, in the back four, almost as if he was hell-bent on proving there was still a shrewdness to his tactical approach. In truth, it was a move that took more away from Forest than it gave, especially as Nigel, with ten goals, was the side's most potent threat.

Clough had decided to retire at the end of the season, but even the timing of that move was taken out of his hands. Chris Wootton, a Forest director, had gone public in two Sunday tabloids with the allegation that Clough's reliance on alcohol had forced the club's hand and they were discussing sacking the manager.

Even as a junior reporter on a local paper, I was aware of the tales of Clough's love of a drink, but it remained one of the great unwritten stories, even if it was discussed in media rooms and press boxes wherever Forest played. Looking back at pre-match television interviews he gave to the likes of Sky, it's impossible to escape the fact that Clough was impaired even before a ball had been kicked. But Wootton's damning indictment destroyed the nod-and-a-wink approach to Clough's boozing; the hare was running, and no amount of crisis management could save him.

With the media massed at the City Ground on the morning of Monday 26 April 1993, Forest organised a board meeting where Wootton, despite pressure from his fellow directors, refused to resign and was suspended. This was duly transmitted to the waiting reporters when, almost as an afterthought, it was revealed that Clough would be retiring at the end of the season. In a fortnight, eighteen years of his labour would be over.

Protestations from the Forest board that Clough's departure had nothing to do with Wootton's accusations were far from convincing. To add salt to the wound, Clough had not told his backroom staff he was quitting, let alone the players, who found out from reporters or on the radio news. There were still two games to play to try to guarantee Forest's Premier League safety and yet here was a man who relished his manipulation of the media over the years now appearing to be hounded out of the club he had built.

For those closest to Clough, anger at the way he had been treated was tempered with relief. John Sadler, who for many years had ghost-written Clough's articles in the *Sun* as well as being an outstanding columnist in his own right, had written an impassioned piece, begging his old friend to go. It was not a betrayal, but a piece written with astonishing compassion. As he told Pat Murphy, 'It was one of the easiest pieces I've ever written. It was no more than I'd said to his face a few times before. I was worried that the game he had given so much distinction to was beginning to destroy him.'

It seems incredible now to look back at those two games. I covered his final match at the City Ground, a 2–0 defeat to Sheffield United that sealed Forest's relegation fate. Yet there was not a single protest from the Forest faithful, the travelling supporters chanted Clough's name and the kick-off was delayed as fans clambered over the advertising hoarding to give him flowers while photographers surrounded him until they were dispersed by a policeman.

And at the end, Clough went on a lap of honour.

Nineteen years earlier, just hours after he was sacked by Leeds United following forty-four tumultuous days, Clough sat in a Yorkshire Television studio alongside his nemesis, Don Revie, the Godfather of Elland Road who had left Leeds to manage England. It remains an astonishing piece of television as these two men, their contempt for each other barely concealed, sniped and snarled for twenty-six minutes of electrifying footage. It was Clough at his bravura best: defiant, charismatic, sharp and so full of life and vigour despite the setback of the sack.

The man who faced Sky's Martin Tyler in the aftermath of the Sheffield United defeat could not have been more different. His face mottled, his hands shaking, there is an attempt to verbally joust with Tyler, yet it comes across as rambling and lacking in linear thought. Only when Tyler asks Clough if he will miss the game does the old fire light in his eyes.

'I'm a football manager by trade, that's my trade and I do it well, I do it good. It could be argued I'm the best in the business.'

Once, that was true. How sad that a man out of time had been ruthlessly exposed by a game to which he had given so much.

7

Bungs, Bribes, Betting and Booze

'I'm the only one in the penalty area at the moment but I won't be for long. It's going to get very crowded.'

With those words, George Graham picked up a crystal tumbler of Scotch, pushed back his chair and breathed a sigh of what seemed like relief. 'Have you got enough, son? Is there anything else you need?'

The stress etched on his face has nothing to do with Arsenal's 1–1 draw with Leicester, even though that has seen the Gunners slide further towards mid-table mediocrity. It's 1995 and we are in the manager's office at Highbury, Graham, his lawyer and me, crafting a piece for the following day's *News of the World* which attempts to explain Graham's role in the biggest corruption case to hit English football.

Exactly a week earlier, I was frantically trying to raise Graham to alert him to an astonishing story that was about to break in the *Mail on Sunday*. The Arsenal manager was about to be very publicly accused of taking 'bungs' from a Norwegian agent totalling £425,500, a cut, it was alleged, from the transfers of Pal Lydersen and John Jensen to the Gunners.

Graham was a columnist at the *News of the World*, con-tracted to write ten pieces throughout the season. The fact he was refusing to pick up either his mobile or his landline did not exactly bode well when one of our biggest rivals was just hours away from landing one of the biggest football stories of the decade.

The Premier League was only in its third season and while the money flooding into the game had seen a sea change in football's finances, the figures the *Mail* were describing still had the capacity to shock. Graham's annual salary at the time was £300,000, comfortably towards the very top of the wage charts, and yet he had received £425,000 MORE in under-the-table payments. To use my sports editor of the time's phraseology, this was a 'fuck me, Doris' story.

I was scrabbling. To be fair to Fred Burcombe, the deputy sports editor at the *News of the World*, he had led the way in January when, with the help of his Scandinavian contacts, he had hinted that there were serious doubts over the transfers of Lydersen and Jensen, that there were discrepancies in the fees received by IK Start and Brondby respectively. But Fred had not been able to nail down the link between Rune Hauge, the agent involved in both deals, and Graham.

Unfortunately for me, Simon Greenberg and Lawrence Lever at the *Mail on Sunday* had made the connection.

In the years before the Premier League, agents were rare creatures who contented themselves with negotiating commercial deals for their clients; sponsored boots, the odd book deal or newspaper column, they were the staples. Transfers were conducted either manager-to-manager or at direct boardroom level and the use of a third party to smooth the deal was still far from the norm. Secret negotiations and side deals felt like the stuff of spy novels rather than football transfers, but a trickle of agents had begun to insinuate themselves into deals, especially when the Premier League started casting an eye overseas for talent. The smart ones linked both buying and selling clubs, providing a trusted concierge service – with Hauge dominating the Scandinavian market in this way.

The first edition of the *Mail* landed in our Wapping office at about 11 p.m. Still without a word from Graham, I was forced to cobble together what was basically a rip-off of their story, being careful not to heap too much criticism on our columnist, relying just on the bare facts. It was a desperately poor piece and far from the high point of my career.

My phone rang at around 9 a.m. on Sunday morning; it was George. 'I understand you were trying to get hold of me last night, judging by all the messages on my phone. Is everything all right?'

All right? He was at the centre of the greatest financial scandal to hit the game, while I was having my backside handed to me by one of our rivals who had scooped us and the rest of the world. To paraphrase a line from *Pulp Fiction*, I was pretty damn far from all right.

Yet Graham seemed perfectly calm, clear-headed and phlegmatic about the whole situation. I arranged to meet him at the Arsenal training ground in Hertfordshire on Tuesday when he would explain everything, and we could plot a way of rebutting the accusations.

How we were going to do that seemed, at that moment, beyond me. Over the next forty-eight hours, more and more facts emerged, facts that made me feel the *News of the World* might be about to attempt to defend the indefensible. Graham had accepted two bungs – and they were always 'bungs' following Alan Sugar's graphic High Court claim against Brian Clough eighteen months earlier – one of £140,500 in December 1991 in bundles of £50 notes and the second in the summer of 1992, via a bank transfer of £285,000, both from Hauge.

The fact the first payment came just six weeks after

Lydersen signed from IK Start, a deal which Graham had personally negotiated, made his claims of 'unsolicited gifts' difficult, if not impossible, to swallow. That he had also repaid the money plus interest to Arsenal over two years later in December 1994 added a fair degree of incredulity to his story.

Why, I asked when we met up, did he hand the money to Arsenal rather than back to Hauge if he honestly believed it was a gift? 'Paul, it just seemed like the right thing to do. I had a meeting with Peter Hill-Wood [Arsenal chairman] and Ken Friar [secretary] in September because they'd heard stories out of Scandinavia about Hauge's methods and they were concerned.'

Incredibly, they were not concerned enough to suspend their manager, even with the evidence against him mounting. But that was the aloofness of Arsenal at the time; with Highbury's fabled marble halls, liveried commissionaires on the door and the bust of Herbert Chapman, Arsenal were the very embodiment of football's establishment elite. Even Graham's office at the ground resembled a gentrified drawing room rather than a working office, with its wood panelling and leather chairs.

It was viewed as impudence of the highest order that the media dared to question why Arsenal refused to suspend Graham or even make a statement. It was made clear this was very much an in-house Arsenal affair and they would not be sullying themselves with something quite so irksome as a press conference or statement.

The degree to which the Arsenal board considered this a trifling incident is underlined by the fact that Graham was allowed to sign three players – John Hartson, Chris Kiwomya and Glenn Helder – less than a month after he had repaid the £425,000 plus £40,00 interest. It beggars belief that a manager under such a degree of suspicion was allowed to carry out his day-to-day duties with barely a question raised.

By the time George and his lawyer ushered me into his office the following Saturday, it felt like the fires were raging out of control. There were whispers on the newspaper grapevine that the *Mail on Sunday* would have further revelations, the Scandinavian media were crawling all over the story and, in the background, the Premier League were carrying out their own investigation which, unbeknownst to Graham, had started two months earlier. Unlike the Football Association, whose disciplinary process moved at a glacial pace, the Premier League employed external law firms and forensic financial experts who were adept at exposing fiduciary malfeasance. They were to be Graham's downfall.

To give George his credit, he had said nothing publicly, respecting his exclusive *News of the World* contract, saving his first words for the paper. We sat for over an hour as he answered question after question. Throughout, he stressed that he considered the two payments as gifts, that he had opened doors for Hauge. For example, content that he had David Seaman and Anders Limpar at Arsenal, Graham had no hesitation in recommending Peter Schmeichel and Andrei Kanchelskis to Manchester United – and was simply being rewarded for introducing Hauge into the upper echelons of so many top clubs. Whether the Arsenal board would have thanked their manager for helping to strengthen a title rival is highly debatable.

He also hinted more darkly that corruption within the English game was even more widespread than anybody suspected, hence his assertion he would not be the only one in the 'penalty area' should the game's authorities decide to truly take a deep dive into football's darkest depths.

Graham's exclusive, it has to be said, was met with

scepticism by the rest of the media and football as a whole. Even the Arsenal board, it seemed, were waking up to the fact that this was no longer a story they could ignore.

For just over a week, with every newspaper and television channel furiously speculating on Graham's future, Arsenal considered their position. There was a split at boardroom level, with the likes of old Etonian chairman Peter Hill-Wood convinced the controversy would blow over while vice-chairman David Dein and some of the more progressive minds among the directors understood the implications of Graham's actions and his relationship with Hauge.

As Graham was preparing for the match against Nottingham Forest on the morning of 21 February, he received word that his presence was required in the boardroom. He told me later that this was not an unusual occurrence and that, having fought his corner over the payments, he suspected he was going to receive a pep talk from the board over the need for results to improve. For once, Graham had been blindsided.

He was not invited to sit down, simply handed a letter informing him of his immediate dismissal and given just a few minutes to clear his desk and make any phone calls needed. He would later be banned for a year by the FA.

Around thirty minutes later, Arsenal issued a statement: 'Arsenal Football Club have been informed by the FA Premier League inquiry of the results of their investigations into the alleged irregularities concerning transfers, and the board have concluded that Mr Graham did not act in the best interests of the club. The board have therefore terminated Mr Graham's contract as manager. The chairman said it was sad that Mr Graham's distinguished career with Arsenal FC should have to end this way and paid tribute to Mr Graham for the success he had brought the club.'

*

For a club with such a reputation for probity and traditional values, Arsenal were playing a leading role in this, the Premier League's first season of sleaze. Just five weeks before his sacking, Graham had sat alongside Paul Merson at a press conference, putting a protective arm around his player's heaving shoulders as Merson detailed the breakdown in his life which had led to cocaine, alcohol and gambling addictions.

The previous November, Merson's downfall had been proclaimed in a series of *Daily Mirror* exclusives in which Merson admitted to losing over £100,000 through his gambling addiction, deadening the pain of the losses, primarily with drink but latterly with cocaine.

Drugs were probably the least significant of his addictions yet made the biggest splash, a symbol of the Premier League's excesses that put too much money in the pockets of players who had no idea how to handle their new-found wealth and fame. The fact Merson would have been an addict had he worked on building sites like so many of his school friends was conveniently overlooked. As he described in his autobiography, 'My brain is wired differently. It helped me on the pitch. Ask the lads at Arsenal, or anywhere I played. It drove them up the wall. They would complain I was always looking for the glory ball. It was like my gambling, my drinking, my drugging. It was risk-taking. I didn't see fear. I could do it and I kept on doing it.'

Now, here he was, having spent six weeks in rehabilitation, being paraded in front of the media by the Football Association so proud that they had helped 'rescue' Merson, barely pausing to think how this level of scrutiny and exposure might impact his already fragile mental state. To be in the room at the Park Court Hotel felt unedifying; when Merson broke down, it all felt so unnecessary.

Merson was a victim of a culture that was born long before

the dawn of the Premier League, one that turned a blind eye to a reliance on booze among players, that passed off obliterated days as 'bonding sessions' and placed a premium on those who could drink as hard as they played, for they were the ones who supposedly fostered the fabled team spirit on which English football thrived. The glittery new world of the Premier League did little to initially change that mentality.

Arsenal's Tuesday Club was the embodiment of that culture. As soon as training finished, a hard-core group led by Tony Adams would adjourn to the pub, credit cards would be left behind the bar and a brutal session would commence, one that would only end when, in Merson's words, he would bump into the milkman. George Graham, like so many of his managerial peers, tolerated its existence without actually condoning it, and the occasional excess – like Adams being jailed for fifty-eight days in 1990 after being convicted of drink-driving – would be forgiven as long as results were not suffering.

For Merson, it was the perfect environment, as he explains: 'It was every Tuesday without fail and the manager loved it because it was team bonding. We'd just get in a bar and we'd sit there all day, then at night it was out to a club and then on to another bar where all the people who worked in bars would go to afterwards and we'd be drinking literally until six or seven in the morning. We weren't in training on Wednesday, so we'd be out again.

'I dread to think what I would drink in a session. Ten pints would be no problem, then it was shorts, but we weren't going in fancy wine bars drinking champagne or anything, it was just normal pubs. There were no mobile phones, no cameras.

'I honestly loved it. If someone said to me, you could play now or you could have played when I played, I would not change. People say, "Oh, what about the money?" The money came and the money went, I would still have been an addict,

HISTORY IS MADE: Steve Bruce and Bryan Robson lift
the first Premier League trophy in May 1993

ARCHITECTS OF HISTORY: David Dein (top), Martin Edwards (middle) and Greg Dyke (bottom) drove the formation of the Premier League

SKY HIGH: Rupert Murdoch and Sam Chisholm redefined television's coverage of football

DEANE AND DUSTED: Brian Deane scores the first goal in Premier League history for Sheffield United versus Manchester United, August 1992

SHAKING THE ESTABLISHMENT: Sir Kenny Dalglish, Ray Harford, Alan Shearer and Jack Walker inspired Blackburn Rovers and changed the face of football

HOW IT BEGAN AND HOW IT (NEARLY) ENDED: Eric Cantona
defined Manchester United's dominance but also courted controversy

SLEAZE CENTRAL: Paul Merson breaks down as he confesses his alcoholism (above). Bruce Grobbelaar on the steps of the High Court

EUROPEAN ROYALTY:
Dennis Bergkamp (left)
and Jurgen Klinsmann
were at the forefront of a
foreign invasion of talent

no matter how much money I was on. I just loved playing when I did.'

But like all addicts, it was only when Merson realised his helplessness in the face of his demons that he reached out. Perversely, it was the media who helped him take his first steps towards relative salvation. While we in the sports pages quietly ignored the life Merson and others were leading off the pitch, thinking we were protecting our contacts, the news pages were not so squeamish. The *Mirror* bought his story, paid him well to cooperate and went loud and proud in November 1994.

'Yeah, the FA weren't too happy with that when I spoke to them but I knew that if I'd just gone to Arsenal and them, they would have said I was injured and hidden me away. I have to face up to things and tell people the truth.

'I was drinking and gambling like a maniac. Then I found cocaine and it just completely changed me, changed the way I was, changed my addiction. From February to that November, I couldn't believe how much it took over my life.

'I'd drive to work nearly every day, thinking, "I'm going to pull over here, pull into a lorry." And it was only the thought of how that lorry driver was going to feel if he hits me and I'm dead that stopped me. He's got to live with that for the rest of his life. But they were the thoughts that were going through my head every day.

'I thought I had to tell somebody, but I thought they'd think I was mad, that they wouldn't let me play football again. I was like a mouse on one of them wheels and it was just spinning. I remember playing against Odense in the Cup Winners' Cup and I thought my heart was going to come out my shirt. I was taking so much of the stuff that my heart was just racing.

'I used to literally go out at night and instead of going home, I'd go straight to training. I went out one night, went to a bar and straight from there to training and I'm snorting in the back of a black cab and the driver was going to me, "What are you doing, son?"

'It got to the point where I went to see Ken Friar [Arsenal secretary] and I said, "I'm struggling here, I feel myself dying I really do." The thoughts in my head, the cocaine. I couldn't get enough of the stuff, even though it was killing me. And he just said I needed to go and see someone, got the FA involved and they brought in this man called Stephen Stevens from The Priory hospital.

'He said, "You've got to come into our treatment centre for six weeks on a programme." I said, "But that's over Christmas, I can't be away from my kids at Christmas." He sat me down and said, "Well, we'll make it very simple, then. Don't come in this Christmas but you won't see next Christmas." And that was it, plain and simple.'

On top of the requirement to undergo treatment and his humiliation in the subsequent press conference, Merson was also banned by the FA until February 1995 when, just a week before Graham's sacking, he was free to face AC Milan in the Super Cup final at Highbury, the first step in his career rehabilitation.

He recalls, 'I came on as substitute and when I ran on to the pitch, I received this round of applause from the fans. I was stood next to Paolo Maldini and he went, "Welcome back," and I was like, "Woah, this story went that far, did it?"'

By the time Merson made his comeback, he was playing second fiddle in the controversy stakes to Eric Cantona, who had usurped him on both the front and the back pages after his Selhurst Park antics.

For a tabloid reporter, those months verged on the surreal. The old mantra for football journalists is that readers want 'mud on boots' coverage – what happened on the pitch, not off it – but the controversies of that season were impossible for any of us to ignore, even if we had wanted to. (And we didn't!)

To underline that point, the first scandal of the season played out in hotel rooms on hidden cameras and secretly recorded conversations and, just as with the George Graham bungs affair, centred on money and the single greatest taboo in English football – match-fixing.

It had been thirty years since Tony Kay, Peter Swan and David 'Bronco' Layne had been jailed for their part in a betting scandal while playing for Sheffield Wednesday. Since then, whatever ills had dogged the game, match-fixing had not played a part. All that was to change in November 1994.

The front page of the *Sun* virtually screamed: Bruce Grobbelaar, Liverpool hero and now playing for Southampton, had, according to his former business partner Christopher Vincent, been involved in fixing five Premier League matches during his time at Anfield and St Mary's. More than that, Wimbledon stars John Fashanu and Hans Segers acted as middle-men and conduits for a Malaysian businessman, Heng Suan Lim, who represented an Asian betting consortium.

It was a story that had all the hallmarks of a tawdry crime thriller. Grobbelaar and Vincent had both invested heavily in a failed game reserve in their native Zimbabwe, leaving the former Liverpool goalkeeper seriously out of pocket but Vincent facing bankruptcy.

Vincent approached the *Sun*, claiming he could get evidence that Grobbelaar had fixed a number of matches and that he was willing to take part in a 'sting' operation involving hidden cameras.

Grobbelaar asserted throughout that he knew Vincent was trying to entrap him, that he suspected his former colleague was in the pay of a newspaper and only went along with the charade to turn the tables on Vincent and expose him as a con man, which he would ultimately report to the police and football's authorities.

For days, the *Sun* was filled with lurid stories of how Grobbelaar had been paid £40,000 to throw Liverpool's game against Newcastle, driving to Fashanu's house to collect the money that had been paid by Lim. Grobbelaar was also caught on film saying he had lost £125,000 by making two fantastic saves, almost by accident, in Liverpool's 3–3 draw with Manchester United. 'I dived the wrong way and it fucking hit my hand,' he was recorded saying.

In February 1994, Grobbelaar and Vincent drove to London to collect £1,500 from Lim the night before Liverpool drew 2–2 at Norwich City, the goalkeeper claiming he would have won £80,000 had his side lost. On Vincent's final recording, he could be seen handing over £2,000 cash to Grobbelaar, now a Southampton player, as a down payment ahead of 3–3 draw against Manchester City, a game in which Grobbelaar claimed he would have earned £50,000 if his side had lost by a single goal.

This was truly the stuff of nightmares for the Premier League. Here they were trying to sell the new golden dream only for it to be tarnished by tales of bribery, backhanders and sleaze. Thankfully for the game's authorities, the police took the matter out of their hands when they charged Grobbelaar, Fashanu, Segers and Lim with conspiracy related to match-fixing in July 1995.

The trial eighteen months later heard that Lin admitted paying Wimbledon goalkeeper Segers £45,000 and Grobbelaar between £8,000 and £9,000 over a period of several months but, crucially for the defendants, only to forecast the results of matches, not to fix them. A jury, seemingly perplexed by the intricacies of the case, failed to reach a verdict, although not before hearing the judge describe Vincent as a 'thoroughly dishonest con man'.

A retrial where, again, all four men pleaded not guilty, ended in exactly the same way, with a jury failing to reach a verdict. The four defendants walked free, with only Grobbelaar facing an FA charge and receiving a £10,000 fine for bringing the game into disrepute.

Fashanu and Segers decided discretion was always the better part of valour and attempted to put the affair behind them. Grobbelaar, though, emboldened by freedom, decided to sue the *Sun* and, after sixteen days in the High Court, was awarded £85,000 with all his legal bills covered by the newspaper.

Wiser counsel may have seen the folly in taking on Rupert Murdoch, and the old adage of never picking a fight with a man who buys ink by the barrel was borne out as a verdict in the House of Lords found in favour of the *Sun* and Grobbelaar saw his award cut to just £1 – the lowest permissible under English law.

So, Graham, Merson, Grobbelaar, England fans rioting in Dublin – forcing the match against Ireland to be cancelled after just twenty-seven minutes – oh, and just for good measure, Chelsea captain, Dennis Wise, found guilty of assaulting a taxi driver and spending a day in prison before his three-month sentence was overturned on appeal.

While the spectacle of the Premier League was undeniable and the football on offer reaching new heights of excellence, it was still mired in seedy grubbiness. The surface may well have been given a shiny gloss but there persisted a dark underbelly of greed and violence.

It felt like the Premier League was in need of a gear change, something – or somebody – that could alter the face of English football irrevocably.

8

French Lessons

On the way back to London from Portman Road, the Arsenal team bus broke down on the side of the A12. Disgruntled players stood huddled on the side of the dual carriageway, most with hands in pockets, few willing to lift their heads as the traffic sped by. Almost two hours after the final whistle of John Wark's testimonial where Arsenal had somehow scraped a draw, it was clear they were going nowhere fast.

A more fitting metaphor for the state of Arsenal Football Club you would struggle to find.

Bruce Rioch had been appointed manager in June 1995 in the aftermath of the George Graham scandal and tasked with not only restoring the club's horribly tarnished reputation but also rebuilding a side that had slumped to twelfth in the Premier League the previous season. It was a challenge that was palpably beyond him.

Yes, results improved, but when your first few signings include Dennis Bergkamp and David Platt, it is clear you have been given both the support of the board and the tools by which to implement a radical overhaul. What Rioch lacked was anything approaching the required man-management skills to convince a talented group of players he was anything but a parade-ground martinet. The Arsenal board thought they had appointed somebody to bring discipline back to the club; instead, all they had found was a man with a small-town mentality, unable to cope with the demands of big-name players.

Rioch's way of impressing Ian Wright, a man for whom respect is everything, was to inform a Golden Boot-winning striker and the player who would lead the Arsenal goal-scoring charts for six seasons running that his game would improve if he watched the kind of runs John McGinlay made for Rioch's previous club, Bolton Wanderers.

As well as being a ludicrous suggestion given Wright's brilliance, it also offended the man whose mood often defined the Arsenal dressing room. Wright rebelled and put in a transfer request. It was rejected and Rioch was told he had to be more flexible in his approach. It was a move that completely undermined the manager's authority and only a matter of time before Rioch was history. On 12 August 1996, two days after being left on the side of the road, Rioch's Arsenal journey was over.

His departure was a vindication for the Gunners' vice-chairman, David Dein. Dein had been staunchly opposed to Rioch's appointment, arguing that simply appointing a poor man's George Graham would barely make an impact, especially when Arsenal were branching out with the quality of European signings like Bergkamp and Platt, who had spent four years in Italy before returning to the Premier League.

Where was the sophistication? Where were the fresh ideas? Where was the vision? Dein, of course, had been an architect of the Premier League and had seen how the money from the Sky broadcast deal was opening doors to Europe, and yet Arsenal's mindset remained firmly entrenched in the past. Dein knew in his heart who should have replaced Graham but he had been overwhelmingly outvoted by the rest of the board. He was not about to lose the same battle.

Seven years earlier, a tall, slightly awkward figure in a trench coat and oversized glasses appeared in the Cocktail Room at Highbury. Even in 1989, women were forbidden to sample the hallowed air of the Directors' Lounge, so it was Dein's wife, Barbara, who extended the first greeting to Arsène Wenger. Dein takes up the story. 'I got the message that Barbara had bumped into the manager of Monaco. I always like to talk to people from overseas to discuss football, so I went through to the Cocktail Lounge and introduced myself. Arsène was just passing through, spending one night in London having flown in from Istanbul before heading back to Monaco, and wanted to take in a game. I asked him what he was doing that night and he replied, nothing. The next question and the answer changed all our lives.

'I said, "My wife and I were going out for dinner tonight, would you like to join us?" He said he'd love to, and that really was the beginning of our relationship, that was the beginning of the love affair.'

Dinner was at a friend of the Deins, and the night ended with a game of charades, Dein communicating via his best A level French. 'Within a few minutes, Arsène was acting out *A Midsummer Night's Dream*, and while I'm not spiritual, I could see in the sky, "Arsène for Arsenal". It was destiny, it was going to happen.'

But like many of the greatest romances, it was a slow-burning affair. Dein would find time to visit Monaco perhaps more often, knowing in his mind that studying how Wenger dealt with the Monaco fans and the media as well as the players was as much of the audition process as results and playing style. A mental dossier was being formed, but the small matter of Arsenal's success meant there was absolutely no appetite for change, especially with two League titles in three years and virtually annual success in cup competitions.

Dein, though, never allowed the candle he carried for Wenger's managerial expertise to expire. Instead, he helped send DHL stocks soaring by having VHS tapes of all Arsenal's games couriered down to the South of France on a weekly basis in order to keep Wenger's interest piqued, the two men then dissecting the performances and personnel over the phone.

With Rioch finally out of the picture and Wenger's extensive video library heaving under the weight of Arsenal tapes, Dein was free to make his move. By that time, Wenger had left Monaco for Japan and Grampus Eight in Nagoya and seemed settled in a new culture with a unique set of experiences to satisfy his curiosity and thirst for self-education. But when the telex machine in his Nagoya apartment whirred into life with a message from London, the chance to put all his plans for Arsenal that had been plotted over the last seven years into practice was too tempting to resist.

'I was a bit surprised when I got a telex back from Japan and it was headed "Lineker",' Dein recalls, 'but Arsène was staying in the house Gary used to have and had inherited his telex machine.' With contact made, Dein was on a mission to convince a board who had recognised the error of their ways with Rioch and were far more amenable to expanding the search for a successor beyond Lancashire mill towns.

Armed with the board's backing, Dein flew out to Japan, only to be faced with another hurdle – Wenger's loyalty and integrity towards his Japanese employers. 'Arsène made it clear he would be loyal to his contract and would not be able to leave immediately. However, there was break clause in it that October so he said that if we could negotiate with Grampus Eight, then he would join us then. There were three of us over there to do the deal initially with the club and then with the chairman of Toyota who owned the club. What I remember mainly is that his office was so big, it felt like you had to take a cab from one side to the other.'

If Wenger had impressed Dein with a game of charades on the first day they met, it was nothing compared to the charade that ensued on the Arsenal party's return from Japan. For around a month, there was no official confirmation that the new manager was Wenger even though the media knew it was the Frenchman and Arsenal knew that the media knew. Even when Patrick Vieira and Remi Garde arrived at Highbury, obviously on Wenger's insistence, the club would not confirm the name of the man who wanted them signed. It got to such a ridiculous stage that before pre-match press conferences held by first Stewart Houston and then Pat Rice, their entrance would be greeted by the assembled reporters chorusing, 'Morning, Arsène.'

Official confirmation of the worst-kept secret in football came on 22 September; Wenger arrived as planned at the start of October. Again, legend has turned his unveiling at the training ground into some kind of magical reveal, as if Dein had pulled off a mystifying sleight of hand to stun and surprise the squad. In fact, Wenger had begun to make tactical alterations to the way he wanted the side to play, implemented by Rice, even before he left Japan.

There is a fallacy that Wenger was an unknown on English shores. He had been touted as potential technical director of the Football Association, he had managed Glenn Hoddle and Mark Hateley in Monaco, and those of us fortunate enough to cover European football were aware of his growing reputation. Even in these pre-internet days, we still had the ability to pick up a phone and speak to journalists in France to get a picture of the new man. Yes, the *Evening Standard*'s headline might have been 'Arsène Who?' on the day he was finally unveiled, but that was more a reflection of fans' bewilderment than a lack of knowledge about who he was.

Speak to any football manager and they will tell you the most difficult part of the job is facing a new squad for the first time. Every workforce is cynical about change at the top, but the fear and suspicion is magnified in football when one man holds the fate of so many employees in his hands. That Arsenal squad was particularly hard-bitten, a band of brothers who had played together, had drunk together and, under Graham, had grown protective of each other's flaws. Now here was a stranger, a foreigner, standing in front of them, telling them he could transform their careers.

Wenger's preparation was undoubtedly flawless and impressive, but without the presence of Tony Adams, he might have fallen. When Wenger arrived, Adams was taking his first tentative steps towards recovery from alcoholism. The Adams of old would, undoubtedly, have led the charge to the pub after training and, over far too many pints, cast scorn on this Frenchman who thought he could teach 'the Arsenal' anything they had never seen before.

There was still scepticism from Adams, for sure. He was far from an instant convert and made his views known to Wenger when he felt the manager was attempting too many changes too quickly. But the Adams of October 1996 was a changed man: fragile, uncertain but now open and willing to accept fresh ideas. As he explained in an interview with Cricinfo in 2019, 'I was six weeks clean and sober, and when the pupil is ready, the teacher appears. If Arsène had come to the club two months before, I don't think he would have lasted. I got the last manager sacked because when the captain is spending more time in the pub than on the training pitch, the coach is let down.'

The squad took their lead from Adams. The respect with which he was held as a leader had been enhanced in an emotional meeting at the training ground just weeks before when the captain revealed the depth of his addiction and the changes he was making in his life. He set the mood and the tone of the dressing room more than even Ian Wright, and if the captain was willing to at least listen, then the others would follow.

If the Wenger approach was alien, then it was soon accepted, as Ray Parlour admits: 'Arsène had doctors coming over, talking to us about our diets and even how to eat. When we drank water, we were told to just sip it instead of gulping it down and then disappearing off to the toilet two minutes later. They were silly little pieces of the jigsaw but if it helps you just two per cent, it could be the difference between playing well or not.

'It was strange for us but we could see Arsène's training methods were so focused and every one of the British players, who weren't used to doing that in respect of their diets and all that, really embraced it. It was, "Let's give him a chance and see where it takes us," because it only takes fifteen or twenty per cent of the lads not to agree and suddenly the dressing room can go a different way.

'It certainly prolonged the careers of Steve Bould, Nigel Winterburn, Lee Dixon, all those lads, doing the right stuff in between games. Recovery was so important to Arsène, making sure we were doing our stretches, getting ready for the next match, it was a real eye-opener to see these foreign methods, I'm not sure anybody in England had ever seen anything like it, it was fantastic to work with.'

While alcohol wasn't specifically banned, it was stripped from the Players' Lounge at Highbury and there were enough savvy players among the Arsenal old guard who realised the

Tuesday Club was no longer appropriate. Not everything Wenger introduced in those first months, though, was met with universal approval. 'Chew to win, can you believe it?' recalls Paul Merson. 'After training, we'd head back to the Sopwell House hotel up the road where we used to get changed, we'd do our stretches and then it was lunch.

'It was chicken, steak, potatoes, raw vegetables, and Arsène would literally go around saying, "Chew to win," You had to chew your food until it was like soup in your mouth and he would stand over us, making sure we were constantly chewing, chewing, chewing, because that aided digestion and made sure you were getting all the goodness out of the food.'

On the pitch, Wenger's first season was a bedding-in exercise of his tactics and methodology. The make-up of the team was still largely formed by the nucleus of the Graham era, especially the dependable back line, although switches in formation and injuries to Adams which limited him to just twenty-eight games contributed to a lack of consistency and Arsenal ultimately finished third behind champions, Manchester United, and Newcastle.

But the Premier League had seen enough to be worried about the impact Wenger was having at Arsenal. British managers were suspicious of the whispers they were hearing about some of the Frenchman's changes and the rumour mill was churning out conspiracy theories at an alarming rate.

So many times, reporters would turn up for pre-match press conferences with opposition bosses and, once the tape recorders had been turned off and notebooks put away, the sniping would start. It felt like there was a huge streak of xenophobia at play when other managers started hinting they had heard Wenger oversaw blood doping or blood spinning at the Arsenal training ground or that there had to be something suspicious about a manager who prescribed vitamins and supplements. It was a sign of nervousness, fear and anger that Wenger did not play the accepted game, never meeting his opposite number for a pre-match chat or a post-match drink.

If word reached Wenger, he cared little. It was a season where the likes of Vieira and Nicolas Anelka – signed in February as the long-term replacement for Wright, who would leave the club at the end of the 1997–98 season – were finding their feet in the Premier League, where the training methods were becoming second nature and where Wenger and Dein were forming a formidable axis behind the scenes.

'I insisted Arsène had a house near where I lived in Totteridge,' Dein recalls. 'We got him a home literally two minutes' walk away, which meant I could see him virtually every day. I would see him in the evenings, and it gave us the opportunity to just talk about the day. Did he need any help? What did he think about certain players? What was on his mind? It was part of the bonding between us and helped to build a trust so that when he identified a player he wanted to buy or sell, he could leave that to me.

'He had to get the boys playing, keep them fit and everything else, but when it came to actually signing the players, we worked together on it but I actually had to do the heavy lifting. That was fine, that's what I enjoyed.

'He is just so highly intelligent. He'll talk about theatre, or philosophy, or politics, or economics. But it's his global knowledge of the game and the players that was a breath of fresh air. It was all very well wanting to be the best team in England, but our ambitions were to be the best team in Europe and for that, Arsène was vital. I just felt he could revolutionise the club and take us to another level.'

It was in the summer of 1997 that Wenger truly made his mark on Arsenal. Pre-season training was in Austria, hidden away from prying eyes and also anything approaching temptation for the players. And if the scenery had changed, so had the methods. 'Normally, we'd find the highest hill in North London and run up and down it,' says Parlour. 'Now we had the ball out from the first day and it was with us every day, which was quite a shock.

'There was always a structure to everything, it was all on the clock and there were three blocks of training. The first block would be pretty easy, just getting yourself back into it after having the summer off. Second block gets a little bit tougher, but by then your body is getting used to playing again and back in the fold. The third block is really hard, playing lots of games in Austria and training twice a day.

'I always remember Arsène saying, "It's not how fit you are on the first day of pre-season but how fit you are on the last day of pre-season" – and we were ready to go from day one, I'd never felt as fit.'

Recruitment was equally strong, with Marc Overmars arriving from Ajax and Wenger going back to Monaco to recruit Emmanuel Petit. Suddenly there was a definite French influence within the dressing room, with Vieira, Petit, Anelka, Gilles Grimandi and Remi Garde. While Wenger's country-men assimilated quickly, there was still a clash of cultures, notably where Petit was concerned, as Parlour explains. 'He would come into training and people would say, "Morning", and he'd just walk straight past us.

'I know there's a language barrier at first, but the lads weren't happy with the way he was conducting himself. The next time it happened, it was, "Right, we'll nail him up against the wall." He was told what the rules were and how he had to abide by them. The next day, he was all "Morning!" to everybody he saw, good as gold. It's just courtesy, saying hello to people, whoever they are.

'Nobody is bigger than the canteen ladies or the chefs.

If they don't prepare our food or give us the best diets, we don't win football matches, simple as that. And Manu had to understand that because the odd "Morning" or whatever goes a long way, it creates a culture.'

The pieces were fitting together. Vieira and Petit formed an understanding in central midfield, Anelka was proving the perfect replacement for Wright, Overmars gave the side pace and Bergkamp, well, Bergkamp was simply sublime. His hat-trick at Leicester in a 3–3 draw included a third goal where he controlled a ball over his shoulder from Platt, took three touches before the ball hit the floor and, with his fourth, tucked it into the corner. It is a goal that Wenger describes as 'perfection' to this day.

That same match, though, included the warning signs that Arsenal were a long way off the perfection the manager sought. Leicester's equaliser six minutes into injury time came as a result of defensive confusion when, previously, the Gunners had been experts at closing out games. They may not have lost a Premier League game until 1 November and even topped the table at the end of September, but Wenger knew they were flattering to deceive.

In the midst of it all, a rivalry was building that would define the first decade of the Premier League. Manchester United may have lost Eric Cantona to retirement in the summer, but the recruitment of Teddy Sheringham from Spurs was proving a masterstroke and the absence of Cantona, once deemed so vital to the United cause, was barely noticed. He was still Eric the King to the United faithful, but princes from the Class of '92 made his loss less acute.

Alex Ferguson had guided his side to the top of the table by November and could have gone four points clear with a victory at Highbury. Defeat for Wenger was unthinkable, and he even went as far as to claim a second defeat of the season would make it 'difficult but not impossible' for them to catch the champions.

The 3–2 win for Arsenal in a thrilling encounter ought to have been the turning point in the season, the opportunity to kick on and go toe-to-toe with United. Instead, the next two games – against Sheffield Wednesday and Liverpool – were both lost, prompting the nearest thing to a revolt Wenger had faced against his methods.

The uprising was led by the English players. They had accepted Wenger's way of never conducting an inquest into a defeat or poor performance when tempers and emotions were running high in the immediate aftermath; they had grown used to a more clinical dissection of a game over video analysis at the beginning of the next week. They knew Wenger demanded clear heads rather than volatility.

In their eyes, however, the loss against Liverpool demanded immediate action. When nothing was said on the Monday and, indeed, the squad were given the next two days off, resentment and anger could not be contained. Pat Rice, who had maintained his role as first team coach, was contacted and told, in no uncertain terms, that a core group of the players were no longer content to be treated with kid gloves, no matter how much Wenger wanted to avoid confrontation. There needed to be a bloodletting.

The squad meeting that Thursday at Sopwell House was brutal. Wenger put it down to players not working hard enough or showing adequate desire; if that was a deliberate ploy to fire a discussion, it worked, although even Wenger could not have been prepared for the level of vitriol about to be unleashed.

Adams, Bould and Platt were the strongest voices. Overmars was singled out for his lack of work-rate, Vieira and Petit accused of neglecting their defensive duties, while

Bergkamp's brilliance was considered too fleeting, too ephemeral, to be of any consistent use to the side. If there was a savagery to some of the criticism, there was also some healthy honesty.

Wenger now concedes that in that first full season, he underestimated the value of the older English players, that he was convinced that as they approached their thirties, they needed to be replaced with fresh minds and bodies. Instead, he learned to trust them and recognise the strength of character they possessed which age did nothing to dilute.

He also played the perfect psychological card with Adams after his captain had been dreadful against Blackburn, packing him off to the South of France to work on the ankle injury that was so obviously hampering him but also to clear his head as he learned to come to terms with a life of sobriety.

The home defeat against Blackburn was the turning point the victory over United should have been. The lessons from the no-holds-barred team meeting were taken on board, Wenger's message of unity was a strong one and there was a steel to Arsenal which even United, for all their flair and experience, could not match.

Twelve points behind United at the end of 1997, Arsenal were immaculate from the turn of the year. A run of eighteen unbeaten games, including eight consecutive clean sheets, reeled in the champions and made a mockery of bookmakers who had paid out on United regaining their crown. If that decision was as insulting as it was ridiculous, Wenger's side underlined their psychological advantage over Ferguson's side with a 1–0 win at Old Trafford. An Overmars winner fifteen minutes from time did not do justice to the dominance of the performance and the momentum of the title race was heading in only one direction.

During that run, it was a pleasure to cover matches at

Arsenal. Be it on a weekend or a night fixture, to emerge from Arsenal underground station, turning left and then right along streets of Victorian terraces before grabbing a first glimpse of the edifice that was Highbury, was a privilege. The football may not have touched the heights of later Arsenal sides; it was the more the realisation that, as a reporter, you were witnessing an elevation of standards both on and off the pitch, a fresh vision, an invigoration of English football.

Wenger and Arsenal had accepted Manchester United's challenge and more than matched it. The title was clinched with two games to spare with a 4–0 win over Everton at Highbury rounded off by the sight of Bould chipping a ball forward with a delicacy that even Bergkamp couldn't conjure, sitting up perfectly for Adams to drive home. Two weeks later at Wembley, Wenger was also clutching the FA Cup as Arsenal won the feted Double.

The snide comments may have persisted from managers whose default setting was protectionism, but the smart ones – the ones left in Wenger's wake less than two years after his arrival in England – were implementing changes. A brigade of doctors, nutritionists, dieticians and sports scientists would soon be commonplace in the Premier League. Yet the head start Arsenal had would stand them in commendable stead over the following seasons.

Wenger had changed the face of Arsenal and English football irrevocably, and we were all the better for it.

9

This Is Your Captain Speaking

'This is your captain speaking, now let's go and get f***ing lamped!'

Anybody who travelled with Arsenal throughout their European Cup Winners' Cup campaigns in 1994 and 1995 would be familiar with that particular refrain. It came from Tony Adams and was directed at all the Arsenal players, staff and well-heeled fans travelling home on the club's private charter from all over the continent.

Reporters who also formed part of the Arsenal entourage remember it all too well. A couple of minutes before take-off, Adams would get to his feet, take the Tannoy and, fresh from another European triumph, begin his rambling message. It was usually prefaced with abuse or snide comments about the media as we sat at the back of the plane, always the last to board after filing our reports, and would always end with a rallying call to oblivion.

What probably failed to register with Adams was the fact that not once were his boorish comments ever publicly reported, that his mantra of 'win or lose, hit the booze' stayed within the confines of the privileged few who accompanied the team on their travels. Because nobody in the press had any intention of exposing the Arsenal captain or the state he usually found himself in at the end of those flights. Looking back, perhaps we played our part in enabling his behaviour.

Because we knew about his drinking. It was difficult not to be aware when it landed him in prison on driving offences, saw him fall down a concrete flight of stairs outside a night-club and split his head open or when he was warned by police after setting off a fire extinguisher in an Essex branch of Pizza Hut.

A passage in his superb autobiography *Addicted* perfectly encapsulates the Adams of that time. In the aftermath of Arsenal's title triumph in 1991, he writes, 'The drinking was no problem. I was doing my job well, we were champions. I did not know I was an alcoholic in development, nor what the price of such an intense way of life was going to be. I was just living on my talent and my instincts, doing my two-fingered best to prove everyone wrong about me and to accumulate trophies for Arsenal.'

And Arsenal protected him, cosseted him even, because the price you paid for having one of the most inspirational captains English football has produced was tolerating Tony's behaviour and too often turning a blind eye. Talking to George Graham in his most unguarded moments revealed a manager torn. Of course, Graham knew the depths to which Adams could sink in drink but he also confessed to fearing that changing the man off the pitch would irrevocably change the player on it.

I remember first seeing Adams when he was sixteen years old and captaining Arsenal's youth team. It was probably less than a year before he made his first-team debut, and it was easy to see why people were talking of him as a future leader of the England side. Even at that young age he was immense, a charismatic figure driving, organising and cajoling those around him, a towering presence in both size and character without a sign of weakness in his game.

Over the years, he grew to personify Arsenal under Graham: professional, obdurate and functional rather than thrilling. The Gunners won two titles in the years before the Premier League but it was as a cup team post-1992 that cemented their position with the 'one–nil to the Arsenal' chant, worn as a badge of honour rather than a reflection of the dour and grinding football that, while successful, won them few admirers outside the red half of North London.

The night in Copenhagen in 1994 when Arsenal won the Cup Winners' Cup was the perfect reflection of what we had come to expect from Arsenal and Adams. They were out-played in virtually every area of the park by a Parma team that included Gianfranco Zola, Tomas Brolin and Faustino Asprilla. Yet Adams was magnificent that night, marshalling his defence, actually physically pushing teammates into posi-tion when his words were not enough, throwing himself into desperate tackles, leading by example. And when Alan Smith's first-half goal proved to be the winner, there was praise even though much of it was grudging.

Not that Adams seemed to care. He delighted in sticking those two fingers up at the media and the outside world, revelling in an almost anti-hero status, living a dissolute life-style but still able to perform on the pitch for both club and country, taking a perverse sense of pride in walking such a tightrope. In his mind, he was infallible. He might slip, but he would never fall.

Until he did.

Word began to filter out that all was not well in his world before the 1996 European Championships hosted in England. Adams and his wife had split up and his drinking episodes were attracting the attention of news reporters who continually received tips from members of the public who had witnessed Adams's excess. Those of us on the sports pages played down the extent of his behaviour, especially when it was made clear by FA sources that Adams was not involved in the riotous pre-tournament scenes in Hong Kong when images of England players pouring shots down each other's throats in the Dentist's Chair were splashed all over the front pages.

That, though, was just downfall delayed. Adams careered out of control in the aftermath of England's exit on penalties to Germany. For almost two months, he stumbled from one nightmarish drinking episode to another, neglecting his health and, as he revealed in his autobiography, throwing his wedding ring in the Thames as his life descended into chaos.

For those of us who had covered his career closely, the sight of Adams at the Arsenal training ground that day in September 1996 was a shock. The day before, he had called his teammates together and admitted to his alcoholism and the fact he was attending meetings of Alcoholics Anonymous. As is always the case in football, the news reached sports desks within a matter of hours and there was an immediate clamour to speak to Adams. A press conference was arranged for the Saturday afternoon.

It was not just his appearance, which was frail and gaunt after too many weeks of not eating properly, it was also the way he appeared to have shrunk as a person. For the first time we witnessed uncertainty in Adams, an apparent questioning of himself as a man and as a footballer. There was not one glimpse of the boorish arrogance which could so often colour interviews with him; this was somebody stripped bare of everything that had once defined him.

And he was so much the better man for it. I had been in the room when Paul Merson broke down in the press conference to announce his addiction issues and that felt like a humiliation, as if publicly parading this shattered figure was enough to assuage football of its guilt at having turned a blind eye to what we all knew was happening in Merson's life. With Adams, it felt different; this was a man in control of himself and the situation. He calmly read a statement and answered a few questions before leaving.

Everything he brought to his game, Adams brought to his sobriety. His new addiction was staying clean, and he tackled this daunting task with the same dedication that had driven him throughout his career. As he points out in his book, the aim for those taking their first steps in recovery is to attend ninety AA meetings in the first ninety days; Adams went to a hundred.

The renaissance in him as a man was astonishing, and never better illustrated than in Tbilisi in Georgia on his return to the England squad. Glenn Hoddle had taken over from Terry Venables post Euro 96 and was a great believer in forgiveness and rehabilitation. In the absence of the injured Alan Shearer, Adams was named captain. Traditionally, the captain and manager face the media the day before a game, although some within the FA's media cohort questioned whether Adams should be put up.

They need not have worried as Adams gave one of the most starkly honest interviews an England player has given, before or since. He confessed to the weakness of character that allowed alcohol to become a crutch on which he depended for a dozen years. He spoke about reaching the bottom of the pit after the European Championships and the fight that he still had in front of him. There is a streak of pure cynicism that runs through too many of us in the media but, listening to Adams that day, no one could fail to have been moved by his humility. It is tempting to call it a magnificent performance but there was no element of a performance, this was Adams in the raw.

The honesty Adams brought to all aspects of his life could be brutal and teammates sometimes bore the brunt of it. The team meeting that many at Arsenal believed was the catalyst for Arsenal's first Double under Arsène Wenger was at the behest of Adams as he recognised the weaknesses and falling standards the new manager had failed to appreciate. Those in the meeting recall the forensic way Adams highlighted both problems and solutions, and if it meant egos being deflated, so be it.

Yes, there was something of the evangelist about Adams in the early days of his recovery and a simple, 'Morning, Tony, how you doing?' was often met with, 'I'm very well but, more importantly, how are you?' The intensity with which the question came could be unnerving and you found yourself stumbling and stuttering, yet there was no doubting the warmth and sincerity of his enquiry.

While there was nothing but admiration for Adams the man in that first season of sobriety, there was a real feeling he had lost something as a player. Perhaps it was his own personal battle to find a balance between new-found serenity and the old, fist-clenched totem that Arsenal players and fans had come to expect over the last dozen years. Certainly, a long-standing ankle injury in the 1997–98 season was taking its toll, and it reached its lowest point with a performance against Blackburn that was as poor as any in his career that long-time Arsenal observers could recall.

Latterly, Adams confessed that he might have to either quit Arsenal or pack in the game altogether rather than continually slipping below the exacting standards he had set for himself. While Adams may still not have been completely convinced by Wenger as a tactician or motivator, there could be no doubting his man-management skills of insight. Wenger gave his captain three weeks and suggested he visit a fitness coach in the South of France. It was a masterstroke as Adams came back physically fit and mentally refreshed for the second half of the season.

To be at Highbury on that beautiful May afternoon in 1998 was to witness a celebration, not just of Arsenal's title triumph but of a man who finally looked at ease with life. Adams had been magnificent in the title run-in, his old, commanding self yet without the anger and fury that so often marked his leadership, and his performance against Everton that Sunday was faultless. That he capped it with Arsenal's fourth goal was a story none of us would have dared write but one that felt perfect.

It was not the goal itself – Adams somehow in acres of space having galloped forward, taking a touch before a thundering left-foot finish – it was the celebration. Eyes closed, face to the Highbury sun, no screaming theatrics, just a look of absolute contentment and satisfaction at a job well done, a life that, at the moment, could not have felt any better.

Later that summer, after England had fallen short in the World Cup, I was walking through Covent Garden when I spotted Adams sitting on his own in the later-afternoon sunshine with just a book and a cappuccino for company. I was unsure whether to stop and talk but he caught my eye and we chatted. I asked him what he was up to, and it transpired that, coincidentally, we were both waiting for our partners before heading off to the ballet at the Royal Opera House. And for the first and only time, I enjoyed a chat about the merits of ballet with a professional footballer.

It may only have been four years since those announcements on a plane's Tannoy but it felt like a lifetime ago.

10

Golden Boy

It is a story with which my daughter regales friends and family to this day: how she won David Beckham's heart long before Posh Spice came on the scene.

To be fair, the story deserves a little context. It was June 1996 and Beckham was part of the England squad playing in the traditional end-of-season tournament in Toulon alongside the likes of his Manchester United teammate Ben Thornley, Lee Bowyer and Richard Rufus from Charlton and Manchester City's Michael Brown. Beckham, though, was the star attraction, having been an integral part of United's Double-winning side, even if his performances were not enough to force him into the England squad for Euro 96.

I had just joined the *Sunday Express* from the *News of the World* and as part of 'welcome package', I had been sent to Rome to cover the Champions League final before flying down to the South of France to cover the Toulon tournament. Frankly, it was the softest of jobs and, such was the relaxed nature of the assignment, the *Express* suggested it would be nice if my wife and daughter enjoyed a week or so in the sunshine.

Little did I know that the stress levels were about to sky-rocket as I combined covering England's matches with trying to nail down Ruud Gullit for a pre-Euros column after the *Express* signed the Dutchman on an exclusive deal for the summer. Gullit, it has to be said, was a complete nightmare to work with. He seemed simply to ignore or forget any arrangements we had made to speak over the phone, with me in France and him in Amsterdam. His agent was powerless to get hold of him and, in a world where mobile phones were the exception rather than the rule, I was stuck in my hotel room for hours on end, trying to track him down.

My daughter, Sophie, was two at the time and, while not exactly a handful, needed entertaining as all two-year-olds tend to do, a task that fell to my wife with me on the hunt for the elusive Dutchman. One afternoon, while my wife and Sophie were playing around the pool, they were approached by Beckham and Thornley.

'We know Paul is stuck in his room,' Beckham said to my wife, 'so we thought it looked like you needed a break. We'll look after your daughter for the afternoon if you want.' It was an offer my wife was never going to refuse, so she sat back on her sunbed and watched Beckham and Thornley play with Sophie in the pool, buy her ice creams and generally treat her like a princess. That was it. Sophie was entranced and every night before we put her to bed, we had to find Beckham so she could give him a kiss goodnight.

It was a gesture of pure class and one that my wife and I genuinely appreciated, a point I made to Alex Ferguson in a letter when I returned from France. He replied that he was delighted two Manchester United players had shown such qualities and that it was what was expected of those representing the club. 'Both boys have been brought up exceptionally well,' Ferguson wrote, 'and I am delighted they have set such high standards for themselves.'

Within the space of two months, Beckham went from the

shy kid, happy to entertain a toddler in the swimming pool for the afternoon, to the Premier League's first global superstar and the man for whom world leaders, Hollywood royalty and business moguls would clamour to have their picture taken alongside, or even bask for a moment or two in the spotlight of that unique Beckham glow, smitten in the same way as an excitable two-year-old.

'He was meant to be a star,' admits Gary Neville. 'David was always somebody who worked hard, loved the club and was committed to training every single day – but he genuinely wanted to be a star. And he coped with it well because he wanted it, he needed it and he didn't just want to be an ordinary football player.'

Beckham's nascent stardom might have been evident to those around him – 'Perfect tracksuit, perfect trainers, perfect hairstyle,' recalls Neville – but there was still a simplicity to his life. In Toulon, he borrowed money from reporters to pay for an excruciatingly high telephone bill that the Football Association refused to subsidise. And when Glenn Hoddle, at that time the England manager-in-waiting, arrived in the team hotel, Beckham, in awe of Hoddle, was the first in line to have his picture taken and a shirt signed.

That all changed on the afternoon of 17 August 1996, with the goal that echoed around the world.

Wimbledon. Selhurst Park. Halfway line. Hapless Neil Sullivan. Even now, over a quarter of a century later, the goal still has the power to astonish. Brian McClair tapping the ball forward is the simplest of preludes, but as he allows the ball to run across his body, you can already see the strategy forming for Beckham, all the memories of his days as a kid with Ridgeway Rovers where he had tried – with some success – the same outrageous attempt.

For Beckham, there are two outstanding memories of the

goal and neither of them involves the execution and outcome. 'I have one picture in my house where the ball is mid-flight and just dropping into the goal. Behind the goal, you can clearly see my mum, my dad and my sister. To have that picture ... it's just a reminder of such a great moment.

'The other thing was walking into the changing room and Eric Cantona came up to me and said, "What a goal!" And that was better than scoring it because we all looked up to Eric, we all knew Eric could do things like that every day of the week if he wanted to, so for him to say that was one of the best moments of my career.

'For the goal, I remember the ball rolling perfectly and I thought, "Why not?" It was instinctively something I knew I'd done so many times as a youth-team player or a Sunday-league player for Ridgeway Rovers. I knew I could strike the ball pretty well; the sun was out, the game was over and I just struck across the ball. It was going far out left and then all of a sudden it started to turn. And I was like, "This has got a chance," because Sullivan was off his line and then I saw it come back in, come back in, drop and ...'

And his life changed in that instant.

Perhaps Alex Ferguson recognised it more quickly than even Beckham himself. Reflecting on the goal, Ferguson said, 'A few minutes before, Jordi Cruyff had tried the same thing, but it went nowhere near. Then, as David tried it, Brian Kidd turned to me and said, "Not him as well," and I said, "Yes, HIM."' Instinctively, Ferguson knew this was a turning point in a young player's life, let alone his career. He ordered Beckham not to speak to reporters, demanding he went straight on the United coach, desperate to control a situation that, ultimately, would be beyond even Ferguson's grasp.

But these were the days of innocence for Beckham, the days of Brylcreem campaigns and tame newspaper columns, a protective blanket thrown around him by both his club and his advisers. He made his England debut against Moldova and, in the build-up, gave his first national press conference. Calm and assured, if obviously nervous, Beckham was smart enough to open up without giving too much away: it was a faultless display.

Yet even that small act riled Ferguson, who did everything in his power short of arriving at England's Bisham Abbey base to drag his young charge away by the scruff of the neck. Ferguson was outraged that the FA would put Beckham in the spotlight and expose him to more publicity, more hype, more potential for distraction. It was to become an all-too-familiar lament.

'Was I prepared for all the attention I was getting? I don't think anything prepares you for media attention,' Beckham concedes. 'But I've been lucky enough to have played in so many different countries and, even in places you've never heard of with millions of people out there, one of the first things people talk to me about is that goal. I don't know whether it made people sit up and look at me as a player more or as an individual, but it made an England manager notice me and take notice of me as a player.

'Back in the day I was making the right decisions, being part of the right brands and I was able to control them. I was able to control what was going on on the field, which was the most important thing, but then being able to do the other stuff off the field and still be in control. I never turned up on a shoot late or with the wrong attitude. I always tried to over-deliver, and I always tried to be polite because that's how I was brought up as a kid. It's what's given me the opportunity to do things all over the world, to be able to travel to China, Japan, different parts of Asia and Europe and do what I do.'

While nothing changed on the pitch, with Beckham

delivering the kind of performances that won him the Professional Footballers' Association Young Player of the Year and helped United to lift their fourth Premier League title, a seismic change in Beckham's personal life and subsequently the perception of English football was on the horizon.

For four months, Posh and Becks kept their relationship out of the public eye, having met in the Chelsea players' lounge in February 1997 with Victoria scribbling her telephone number on a train ticket. Low-key meetings at her parents' house whenever Beckham had a day off from training, snatched kisses in car parks, safely hidden from the threat of a photographer's lens; again, it was the stuff of more innocent times, just a young couple getting to know each other. It was never going to last.

It is impossible to overestimate the cultural impact and significance of the Spice Girls at that time. By the time David and Victoria met, the group had notched up four UK number one singles, a US number one with 'Wannabe', sold over five million albums and attracted over half a million people to Oxford Street when they turned on the Christmas lights. In 1997, they had the biggest selling album in America and three Brit awards, making them the most successful British band since The Beatles.

Even Beckham, with brands falling over themselves to attach their name to his, was stunned. 'Their global status and stardom was nothing that I'd ever seen before. At the time people did find out about us dating, there was no social media and no camera phones, but whenever we were pictured, it was blown up on so many different levels.

'It probably looked like I was going to more parties and seeing Victoria more than I actually was, just because wherever we went, there was a barrage of photographers. As a young kid and someone who was dating a Spice Girl, I never

let anything at any point get in the way of my career, training or playing, and Victoria was part of that. She knew how
committed I was to Manchester United.'

Not that Ferguson was convinced. Gary Neville, ever
loyal to both the club that nurtured him and his best friend,
could see both sides. 'Sir Alex was just one hundred per cent
Manchester United with football blinkers on. He didn't want
anything outside of that from the point of view of noise,
media intrusion or distractions.

'For him, David was a massively important player, but a
lot of the papers would always have stories about David and
Victoria, and I think Sir Alex saw that as potentially a challenge to David's football performance. It just went completely
to another level because the Spice Girls were taking over the
world and Manchester United were winning and both those
worlds clashed. I would say it was out of control from a media
perspective.

'David and Victoria were in control of their lives but one's
a consistent lifestyle and one's a very inconsistent lifestyle and
I remember being alongside him in that time when Victoria
was touring, and he was playing for United, and they weren't
together. He would travel to London sometimes to catch an
hour [with her]. I remember he was caught at a movie pre-
miere a couple of nights before a game so that was going to
cause tension.'

It has to be said that for all the astonishing scrutiny they
were under, the couple made very few public missteps. They
may have courted a degree of publicity by being seen at all
the right restaurants and events, but their lifestyle was never
dissolute, never shocking, just glamorous and befitting that of
the most famous couple in Britain. It may not have been the
monastic life Ferguson would have preferred but it was largely
beyond reproach.

Not that it mattered; Ferguson could always find a reason to criticise, as Beckham recalls. 'I remember driving past the Trafford Centre a few hours after training and my phone rang.

'"David, it's the Boss. Where are you?"

'"Boss, I'm in my car driving past the Trafford Centre."

'"You're lying to me. My friend is sat opposite you in Barcelona airport, why are you there?"

'"Boss, I'm in my car literally driving past the Trafford Centre."

'"I don't believe you." And then the phone went down. Unfortunately, those were the things that were happening at the time Victoria and I were dating.'

The same fears and suspicion Ferguson had about the relationship impacting on Beckham's football were unfortunately shared by Hoddle for England, despite the fact his performances for club and country rarely fell below the high standards he had set himself. It is almost too easy to dismiss Beckham's playing career and reflect only on his celebrity status, but there were occasions when he was pivotal to everything United achieved with his passing range. He is still the only England player I have seen receive a standing ovation from a press box full of journalists (after his performance against Greece at Old Trafford in 2005).

To those of us covering England at the time, Hoddle's treatment of Beckham at the World Cup was mystifying. Here was a rare talent, perhaps the most gifted passer the English game had seen since Hoddle himself, yet it felt like there was no warmth in the relationship. Whispers within the FA's media team suggested there was a jealousy that Hoddle felt, a resentment at the kind of attention Beckham received from the media.

It was difficult not to foist the spotlight on him. His relationship with Victoria notwithstanding, his ability with a dead ball, pinpoint crossing accuracy, a range of passing beyond anybody else in the Premier League and an eye for the spectacular made Beckham a singular talent with a technique to match the very best in the world.

He played in every one of England's 1998 World Cup qualifying matches, and while not finding the back of the net, had done enough to convince Hoddle he deserved a place in the squad for France. That concession was to be the high point of their relationship.

Engaged five months earlier, it was inevitable Beckham and Victoria would be the focus of attention at the tournament. Locked away on a golf course outside the seaside town of La Baule, the England squad were given little time to be with their partners and families before the tournament proper kicked off. When there was any downtime to be enjoyed, Victoria would fly in and immediately be engulfed in a swarm of photographers and news journalists, all desperate for an exclusive picture or a snippet of gossip.

It was as if that was the excuse Hoddle was looking for. He had already taken the extraordinary step of humiliating Beckham in front of the squad, denigrating his technical ability at free kicks before stepping up himself to show the players how he wanted it executed. Now it felt personal.

'It was a bad situation,' Neville recalls. 'In the lead-up to the World Cup, the manager said he [Beckham] was distracted because of Victoria, because David wanted to see Victoria, which I didn't think was particularly right at the time.'

Nothing anybody could say would change Hoddle's opinion that the United man had completely lost focus, and Beckham was left out for the first game against Tunisia and the defeat by Romania in the next match, which left England's qualification dependent on a win against Colombia in the third and final group game.

Hoddle swallowed his pride, never an easy thing for him to do, and Beckham was recalled. After thirty minutes he rifled in England's second goal with a trademark 25-yard free kick which curled deliciously past the Colombian goalkeeper. It was exquisitely delivered – an act of defiance. His rehabilitation was to be short-lived.

How Beckham survived the onslaught and outpouring of hatred after his red card against Argentina for a petulant swipe at Diego Simeone is difficult to fathom. I was part of the press pack in the tunnel after the game in St Etienne and when Beckham emerged, I have never seen a player look so broken. His eyes were red rimmed with tears; he was shrunken and shell-shocked, with the thousand-yard stare of a man who simply cannot comprehend how his world has been destroyed.

Yet from the embers of that disastrous night, his relationship with Ferguson was rejuvenated, the United manager using the country's animosity towards Beckham as the ultimate psychological weapon in his armoury.

A full appreciation of the Treble season is elsewhere in this book, but the seeds of that success were sown by Ferguson from almost the moment Beckham flicked out at Simeone. After joining Victoria in America to escape the ferocious glare of the English media and public, Beckham was brought back into the Old Trafford fold, offered protection and support he would never find elsewhere and, with it, forged a mindset that would see United revered for the greatest achievement in English football.

'We were wounded by Arsenal winning the Double the year before,' Neville reflects. 'Obviously the manager reacted by signing Jaap Stam and Dwight Yorke, but the other thing was David coming back off the World Cup. The manager built a siege mentality off the back of that.

'You know, everyone hated United, and everyone hated

David Beckham. The idea that he would be booed in every away ground suited Sir Alex and suited us because generally we didn't mind not being liked. If you're not liked, if you are booed, it's the biggest compliment you can be paid because they're worried about you, people are affected by you. And you're in people's heads.'

But if Ferguson had used the antipathy towards Beckham as the glue to help bond the squad in the Treble season, the old frustrations at a lack of control on the manager's part began to surface in the following season, just a few months after the Beckhams were married in July 1999.

Beckham did himself no favours by asking for time off to look after his son, Brooklyn, who was suffering from gastroenteritis only for Victoria to be photographed at London Fashion Week. To Ferguson, it was the ultimate betrayal, missing training and letting down his teammates; it was the beginning of the end.

In his autobiography, Ferguson wrote, '[Beckham] was never a problem until he got married. He used to go into work with the academy coaches at night-time, he was a fantastic young lad. Getting married into that entertainment scene was a difficult thing – from that moment, his life was never going to be the same. He is such a big celebrity; football is only a small part.'

If there is any animosity on Beckham's part, he has never discussed it publicly and the fractured relationship has fully healed, although it needed the move away from Old Trafford to illustrate what both men were probably missing. Without United and Fergie, Beckham would surely have still been an outstanding player but without the greatest stage on which to display his talent. For United, Beckham was not only a magnificent presence on the pitch but also a magnet for global brands who wanted to attach themselves to the club's history and the sheer glamour a superstar personality delivers. It was the perfect combination.

More than anything, the Premier League benefited. From that first broadcast deal of £304 million in 1992, to an astonishing second contract in 1997 which more than doubled the original sum, Sky were paying £1.1 billion by the time Beckham left England for Real Madrid, in no small part due to his global allure. The reach of the Premier League still leaves Beckham more than a little astonished.

'I've travelled to many places around the world and one of the first trips I went on (as a UNICEF ambassador) we went into different villages, met different families, different communities, different kids, and they're all running around in Manchester United shirts and different teams from the Premier League.

'There's maybe one television in every five villages so they rely on the radio. These kids were excited to see me, but it wasn't because they knew my face, it was about what they had heard on the radio. They didn't recognise my face, but they recognised my name.

'There are certain things I've done in my life where I've realised how big football is and it began for me with Manchester United, a team that I always wanted to play for, a team that me and my dad supported our whole lives. When I moved to the US, Tom Cruise threw a party for us, and there was Tom and Will Smith and a young Rihanna and Stevie Wonder – and it was one of those moments where it all came from what I'd done throughout my career playing for Manchester United, being in the biggest league in the world and being there almost from the start.

'When I first moved to Los Angeles, I was able to go to the Lakers every week. This one time, I was really excited because I was in the VIP lounge, and I went to use the toilet. There was a bit of a queue, and I was waiting to go in and all of the sudden, the door opened, and Jack Nicholson walked out. And he was, like, "Hello, David, how are you doing? How are Man United doing?"

'Here you have a Hollywood superstar legend come out of the toilet and, one, I can't believe he recognised me and knew my name. Second, the fact he mentioned Manchester United. That's when you recognise just how big the Premier League is around the world.'

11

The Eternal Optimist

'It's quite a simple thing really. Newcastle fans work hard all week, they want to go and have a couple of brown ales, they go to the match, and they want to see a team in black and white give everything they've got to win a football match and to entertain them.'

If only life was truly that simple. If it was, then Kevin Keegan would surely still be manager of Newcastle United. Because he could entertain, it was in his blood, but what he could never do was deal with expectation: the expectation he put on himself.

Two years after walking away from St James' Park, Keegan was appointed England manager on a wave of public goodwill, fans thrilled by the prospect of the national side playing with flair, elan and a smile on its face. Sitting before the assembled media, he told us that if we were looking for a manager to get England a 0–0 draw, then he was not the man for the job. It should have been a triumphant underlining of his determination to play the kind of football the country craved. Instead, it set alarm bells ringing.

It was the get-out clause, the excuse that Keegan could cling to when, inevitably, the tide turned against him, and self-doubt shredded his natural ebullience. Less than two years later, he was gone, rain-drenched and quitting in the toilets at Wembley, another dream shattered, another vow broken.

Keegan cares too much. The burden is too great for him to bear when things go wrong, or he even senses they are about to go wrong. Criticise him for his tactical naivety or his warped football philosophy, but never question his desire to please or put a smile on a fan's face. Newcastle in their pomp under Keegan were a thrilling, coruscating joyride of a team and a pleasure to cover as a reporter.

They were just never winners.

Does that matter to supporters? Well, yes. Especially when Newcastle under Keegan were shattering the world transfer record to sign £15 million Alan Shearer or thought nothing of £6 million for Les Ferdinand or £7 million for Faustino Asprilla. It's a romantic notion that the Toon Army just want a few bevvies and a bit of fun on Saturday afternoon, but actually they deserved far more under Keegan.

They would flood to St James' Park out of love and loyalty, but where was their reward? They did not deserve to see their team squander a twelve-point lead over Manchester United and finish four points behind the champions. They did not deserve a side that could obliterate United one week and meekly surrender to Leicester the next – and Keegan knew it. He knew that failure, for all the fine words, was never truly an option.

More than twenty-five years after Keegan's first exit from Newcastle (well, second if you include the fit of pique that saw him walk out in 1992 before walking back in after winning a battle with the board a few days later) you can see the truth of the matter. With petrochemical billions behind them, Geordies simply want to win; they care little for style, they demand substance.

Under Keegan, there was plenty of the former but little of

the latter. The team he built in the 1995–96 season was the most exciting the Premier League had seen, a combination of free-wheeling attack and seat-of-the-pants defence, with the manager at the very heart of it, feeding off the highs and desperately trying to ignore the lows.

The template had been set in the shadows of the Premier League's initial season, well away from the grandeur of the top flight, at places like Southend, Tranmere and Grimsby. Keegan had returned to the club he served in the last two years of his playing career and saved Newcastle from the ignominy of relegation to the third tier of the English game. A year later, his side were First Division champions.

And in some style. They won their first eleven games of the season and five in a row to close the campaign, finishing eight points clear of second-place West Ham with a positive goal difference of 54. They finished the season in astonishing style, beating Leicester 7–1, with Andy Cole, for whom they paid Bristol City £1.75 million in March, helping himself to a hat-trick. Truly, it was sign of things to come.

The fact Keegan had actually quit in March 1992 over a perceived lack of backing by the board in the transfer market was conveniently forgotten or, at least, overlooked. Keegan was the Geordie messiah as far as the fans were concerned, a man whose grandfather had been a Durham miner, who had tapped into the heartbeat of Newcastle as a player and had now led the club and city back to the promised land of the Premier League.

Keegan was not above manipulating the emotions of the adoring masses. When he wanted to bring Peter Beardsley back to Tyneside but was being thwarted again by a board who could see little sense in paying £1.5 million for a thirty-year-old, the manager let it be known that Sunderland were also in the hunt for the player. Keegan knew there was no truth in it, the Newcastle board knew there was no truth in it, but, faced with outrage from fans that Beardsley, a true son of the city, could end up with their hated rivals, chairman Sir John Hall succumbed and wrote a cheque to Everton.

It was Sky's Richard Keys who dubbed Newcastle 'The Entertainers' that first season back, after a run of four wins in October and November saw them score fourteen goals and concede just one. It was seized on by the fans who hailed Keegan's side and the goal-scoring prowess of Cole, worn as a badge of honour by the Toon Army and gobbled up by headline writers who recognised a bandwagon when they saw one.

Cole would end the season with forty-one goals in all competitions, thirty-four of them in the Premier League, as Newcastle finished a hugely creditable third and qualified for the UEFA Cup with a brand of attacking flair and panache that underpinned Keegan's philosophy of giving the fans what they wanted. Even if there was a gulf of fifteen points between them and Manchester United, it was a campaign where Keegan's side outscored the champions and there is an argument to say they are the best side ever to have been promoted to the Premier League. For those looking for omens, though, they also conceded the most goals out of all the top five.

The man who wears the number nine shirt for Newcastle is assured of his place in Tyneside legend. When that man also outscores the rest of the country's strikers, they tend to build statues to them on Tyneside. The fact Cole's name is, to this day, treated with disdain at Newcastle is down to only one man. Only one man could sell Newcastle's leading marksman and convince the Geordie faithful that this was part of intricate strategy, a shrewd plan conceived by a manager with vision and foresight for what was best for Newcastle United.

Or could it have just been a fit of pique on Keegan's part because he had fallen out with Cole and saw the prospect of a British transfer record as a salve in the face of righteous indignation?

In essence, it was a little of both. In interviews over the last few years, Cole highlights a series of disagreements between himself and Keegan over the way the manager spoke to Cole's close friend at the club, Lee Clarke. He also resented being told to 'do one' by Keegan after the pair clashed at the team hotel.

For his part, Keegan saw a decline in Cole's performances on the pitch and a series of injuries that he believed was diluting his potency in front of goal. In the background, there was always the feeling Cole had had his head turned by rumours of Manchester United's interest – that, in the parlance of the dressing room, he was 'playing for an away'. A run of nine league games without a Cole goal convinced Keegan and the board that buying somebody to help the striker out of his rut was futile and that it was time for a fresh approach.

Alex Ferguson admitted he was 'shocked' when he was told United had the chance to land Cole. Multiply that shock a hundred-fold and you are probably closer to the feeling among Newcastle fans. As news of the £6 million deal involving £5 million cash and a swap for Keith Gillespie broke in the city, outraged supporters laid siege to St James' Park, gathering around the main reception and demanding answers that only one man could give them.

In his 2018 autobiography, Keegan admits, 'I wasn't prepared to go into hiding. All they [the fans] wanted was an explanation. They wanted to know why and I'm going down to tell them.' What followed was an impassioned plea for patience and understanding, that this was a strategy, not a gamble, and that Keegan would carry the can if the move backfired. Or, in words dripping with the kind of raw emotion he always favoured, 'There's a bullet with my name on it if this goes wrong.'

There was no need for such melodramatics because, for once, both Newcastle manager and board were in complete harmony. Despite the fact Cole had scored a goal every other game before his transfer, Sir John Hall recognised the ability to reinvest spoke louder than Cole's goals. 'We would be rightly lynched if this money was just taken to the bank,' he said just days after the transfer. 'But it will be used to build something special for Newcastle fans. When we have won the Premier League and Champions League many times and built a dynasty, then perhaps the fans will recognise the reasons behind our decision.'

Thankfully for Keegan and Hall, such grandiose words and sentiments helped ease the pain of not only Cole's departure but the fact they finished a hugely disappointing sixth at the end of the season, having topped the Premier League in October. Promises had been made, expectations raised, and the air in the city was heady with hope and belief, just the way Keegan liked it.

To give Sir John his due, he was as good as his word in terms of reinvestment. He sanctioned a £9 million move for Roberto Baggio at Juventus who, at the time, was considered the best player in the world. A fax was sent with an official bid and a three-man deputation of vice-chairman Freddy Shepherd, chief executive Freddie Fletcher and Hall's director son, Douglas, flew to Turin to negotiate without an official meeting having been arranged or even a tacit understanding Baggio was actually for sale, other than agent gossip. The fact nobody at Juventus even entered into discussions did nothing to dampen the mood on Tyneside, it was simply on to the next targets.

Within the space of three days, Keegan had twice broken

the club's transfer record, paying Wimbledon £4 million for Warren Barton and then paying Queens Park Rangers £6 million for striker Les Ferdinand, deemed a more than suitable replacement for Cole. Throw another £2.5 million into the mix for David Ginola and almost £2 million for goalkeeper Shaka Hislop – it amounted to the biggest single spending spree seen in the Premier League.

What does that kind of money buy you? Brilliance and an unquenchable spirit, it would seem. Newcastle lost only two games between the start of the season in August 1995 and Christmas but, as much as the results, it was a harmony off the pitch that helped make them such an irresistible force, as Keith Gillespie explains. 'We gelled, both on and off the pitch. We were very big on the bonding in terms of socialising together. We'd have gone out maybe every three weeks and you weren't allowed not to go, physios, kit men, everybody except Kevin, Terry McDermott and Arthur Cox.'

Ferdinand had inherited both the number nine shirt and the legendary status conferred on Newcastle strikers; it was a mantle he was only too comfortable with. 'It was a dream. You had Ginola who was close to being European Footballer of the Year that first season and he'd cross, and I'd score and take all the glory, but he was incredible ... sensational.

'Keith Gillespie was just out and out pace, get down the line, cross the ball no nonsense. And anybody who has ever played with Peter Beardsley will probably tell you he's the best they've ever played with. He got just as much pleasure out of making a goal as he did scoring himself.

'So, I'd arrived at a club that was all-out attack and for a centre forward, it was a dream come true. For everybody that watched us, we were probably their second favourite team because there was going to be goals one way or another. Yes, we lived up to "the entertainers" but it was just a brand of football that everybody enjoyed, and everybody wanted us to win the title because of it.

'And the fans were incredible, thirty-six thousand every home game. The first time at St James' Park as a player, Lee Clarke and Steve Watson, a couple of Geordie boys, told me that when I go down the tunnel and on to the pitch, that I won't walk, I'll float out on to the pitch because the noise that will come out of the place will be unbelievable. They were as good as their word.

'When I scored (on my debut) I realised what wearing the number nine shirt meant to all the Geordie supporters because if there had been a roof on the stadium, it would have been blown off with the euphoria. That's when I realised what this club was all about.' One thing Ferdinand also recognised was the fact Keegan's team could only play one way. 'I went to a club that was all-out attack. I think our problem was that we probably didn't have any tactics, the only tactic was to attack.'

Not that it mattered before Christmas when they opened up a ten-point gap over Manchester United. Even a 2–0 defeat at Old Trafford the day after Boxing Day, which Keegan described as 'The circus came to town but without the lions and tigers', was seen as a minor blip, especially when the lead became twelve points by 20 January with just fifteen games to play. Two years earlier, when Newcastle confirmed their promotion to the Premier League, Keegan had told the world his side were 'coming for Liverpool and Manchester United'. There are probably many quotes that come back to haunt Keegan, this ought to be one of them.

Gary Neville describes playing for Manchester United as 'like being on an island in the middle of the ocean, you were just on it and no one else could get near it, that's how Sir Alex made you feel'. If United were an island in the second half of the season, then Newcastle were a ship holed below the water line with all the pumps failing and a captain unable to navigate a path to safety.

Whereas Ferguson and United were able to welcome back Eric Cantona from suspension in October, Keegan's decision to freshen his own squad would see the whole season begin to unravel. David Batty was a stout English yeoman and a fine character to have around, but he was not a game-changer. That responsibility fell to Faustino Asprilla.

The Colombian certainly fitted the bill of maverick showman and his debut performance from the bench against Middlesbrough saw him set up an equaliser for Watson before Ferdinand grabbed a winner. Yet for all his talent, Asprilla completely destroyed the balance of the Newcastle attack. Gillespie on the right, with his direct approach, was always the perfect foil for Ginola's elaboration on the left. With Asprilla now keeping Gillespie out of the side – understandable when he cost £7.5 million from Parma – there was barely an early ball into the box for Ferdinand to attack. Frankly, he did not even know if a cross was coming in, let alone when.

From Asprilla's debut on 10 February to 3 April, Newcastle won just once in six games – and the sixth game was when the die was cast, not just for the season but for Keegan's tenure on Tyneside.

An undeserved defeat at home to Manchester United via a Cantona winner meant the Newcastle lead at the top was just a point, yet the situation was far from irreparable; all it needed was calm heads and a realisation that any points gained at this stage of the season were golden. You may as well have told Keegan to fly to the moon.

The match against Liverpool at Anfield will go down not just as one of the best the Premier League has ever seen, but as one of the finest witnessed in the history of English football. Watching it back even now is an exhausting experience, a game to heighten the senses with every pulsating turn, as Liverpool only led twice in the game. But it was that last goal from Stan Collymore for 4–3 that saw Keegan slumped over a wall in front of the dugout, destroyed emotionally, seemingly unable to comprehend what he had just witnessed.

'We've lost nothing in defeat,' was his response – and he may have believed that. But those in the Newcastle dressing room who sat with their heads bowed knew their manager was deluded if he did not realise this was the end, seven games before the season's climax.

'I'll never be at peace with that day until I'm taking my last breath,' Ferdinand admits. 'It's the one recurring nightmare I have. There are pivotal games in a season, in your career, where you look back and think, "What could we have done differently?" If we were a bit more tactically aware, perhaps we would have won the league, but I don't think Kevin would have changed anything because it was his style, it's what he knew the punters wanted to watch and that's what we gave them.

'We were all sitting, having gone away from home and scored three goals and still lost the game and no one said anything. Even when Kevin came in, he sat on the side and said, "What can I say? How can I have a go at anyone? You're playing the type of football I want to see you play. It's just been an amazing game of football and we've come out the wrong side of it."

'I think had we won that game, we would have gone anywhere and won after that, that would have given us the momentum we needed. Instead, that game drained us.'

Such was the impact of defeat at Liverpool that Ferguson probably had no need to turn the psychological screw – but when has that ever stopped him? Ferguson's accusation that the whole of the football world wanted Newcastle to win the title was one thing, suggesting Leeds United were cheating their manager, Howard Wilkinson, by raising their game solely for United was another. Finally, hinting Newcastle would find it easy against Nottingham Forest because the two clubs would meet again for Stuart Pearce's testimonial destroyed Keegan.

He can laugh about it now. He can laugh when his son-in-law presents him with a Manchester United shirt with 'I Would Love It' emblazoned on the back. It even forms part of Keegan's after-dinner shtick, with a nod and a wink and a chuckle.

Yet on the night of 29 April, after Newcastle had beaten Leeds 1–0, there was nothing remotely humorous about it; it was painful, almost too painful, to watch as, post-match, Keegan was gently prodded by Richard Keys and Andy Gray from the Sky studios in London into Keegan's headphones at Elland Road.

As a journalist, you can have nothing but admiration for Keys and the way he manoeuvres the conversation around to Ferguson's comments. It is conversational, not confrontational, yet all the while Keys senses the tension building in Keegan until there is only one escape valve for his anger. Is it worth recounting here? Absolutely.

'A lot of things have been said over the last few days, a lot of it almost slanderous. We've never commented ... but when you do that about footballers and what he (Ferguson) said about Leeds and things like that about Stuart Pearce ... I've kept really quiet, but he went down in my estimation after that.

'We haven't resorted to that, but you can tell him we're still fighting for this title and he's got to go to Middlesbrough and get something.

'I'll tell you honestly, I will love it if we beat them, love it.'

To the outside world, it was a disintegration, as close as a football manager has come to a breakdown live on television. To the Newcastle players, it was a sign their manager was, as he said, still fighting. As Ferdinand explains: 'I don't think there was any of the players that thought, "Oh, Kevin's melted here, he's got caught up in the mind games." We were with him every day and he was very passionate about what he did and the way he did it. I never saw it as losing the plot, I just thought, "Good on him."'

Over in Manchester, Gary Neville had a different view. 'You smell the sort of fear in the other team. You think, "Is it determination? Desperation?" But Sir Alex absolutely loved it if he could smell a little bit of weakness in the opposition and he would exploit it. It sounds crazy but Newcastle were too emotional, you have got to be ice cold. There was too much emotion, too much fever, too much anxiety and excitement.'

Whatever the thought process, the futility of Keegan's railing against the inevitable was exposed when Newcastle failed to beat either Forest or Spurs in their final two matches, leaving United to coast home against Middlesbrough to win the league by four points. In his book *Geordie Messiah*, veteran Newcastle reporter Alan Oliver claims Keegan offered his resignation the night before the last game of the season. While it was denied at the time by the Newcastle board, it would explain much of what unfolded the next season.

When fifteen thousand fans rocked up at St James' Park to hail the return of Alan Shearer for a world-record £15 million, it should have been a cause for celebration. When Philippe Albert strode imperiously forward to chip Peter Schmeichel for Newcastle's fifth goal in a rout of the champions, it ought to have been cause for something approaching delirium. Instead, the joy seemed to have been sapped out of Keegan.

For a start, he had abandoned his routine of daily press

briefing, something by which he had stood since returning in 1992. Now, where once there was effervescence, there was an almost wounded soldier's stance, as if the burden of caring so much was taking the heaviest of tolls. Two defeats in the opening three matches convinced the bookmakers something was intrinsically wrong at Newcastle and the odds on Keegan becoming the first victim of the sack race were cut.

Seven straight wins, culminating in the humiliation of Manchester United on 20 October were a sign that there was still delight to be taken from Newcastle's performances, and a 7–1 hammering of Spurs over Christmas was as comprehensive a victory as I have ever seen in the Premier League. Yet afterwards, Keegan did not attend the post-match press conference. While it was not the biggest issue given the story on the night was all about Tottenham's capitulation, seasoned Newcastle observers sensed everything was far from settled at the club.

Newcastle were in the process of a stock market flotation and the stability of Keegan's position was essential, yet it was apparent the manager had lost the fire in his belly. For his part, Keegan believed the board had lost focus, concentrating almost solely on the flotation of the club with the team becoming of secondary importance. It was a stand-off that neither side needed or wanted, but yet again conflict at the highest level was threatening the stability of the club.

So often Keegan had forced the issue, getting what he needed from a hierarchy who could never contemplate losing him. This time, there was a weakness in his position which owed everything to results on the pitch – and the board exploited it.

Keegan had been willing to see out the season and then walk away – he had even shaken hands with vice-chairman Shepherd on that basis – but that was no longer an option;

either he signed a long-term deal that had been mooted the previous summer and give prospective investors peace of mind or he should go immediately.

On 5 January, the *Sunday Mirror* led their back page with Keegan quitting. It was neither confirmed nor denied by the club, and Keegan himself, in his post-match press conference at Charlton the same day, claimed he was there to talk only about the game, not speculation over his future.

Two days of silence were followed by a story in the *Newcastle Evening Chronicle* on the afternoon of 7 January with the simplest yet most shocking of opening paragraphs: 'Kevin Keegan sensationally resigned today as manager of Newcastle United'.

'I feel I have taken the club as far as I can.' The great entertainer had lost his smile, and the Premier League, for all Keegan's faults, was poorer for his absence.

12

Spice of Life

Blame Neil Harman. As chief football writer for the *Daily Mail*, he was the first to coin the phrase and from there it became tabloid shorthand for excess, for the frittering of talent, for the ultimate example of style over substance.

The Spice Boys.

Mention that moniker to the likes of Jamie Redknapp, Robbie Fowler, David James, Steve McManaman and the other Liverpool players who were all tarred by the Spice Boys brush and their instant reaction is generally, 'Yeah, but ...'

Yeah, but ... we weren't the only ones.

Yeah, but ... nobody ever mentions Ryan Giggs or Lee Sharpe.

Yeah, but ... we were never out forty-eight hours before a game.

Yeah, but ... nobody would have said a word if we had won something.

And in that final line is the absolute kernel of truth. If Liverpool had won a meaningful trophy other than a single League Cup in the last decade of the twentieth century, Harman and the rest of us in the sports pages would not have raised an eyebrow at the white suits and the nights out. We would have paid tribute to the finest group of young players assembled in those early Premier League years and we would be talking about an Anfield dynasty continued.

Because, make no mistake, in terms of sheer talent, I would have taken Liverpool's squad over Manchester United's every day. How could you not be beguiled by the likes of Fowler and McManaman? How could you not marvel at the beauty of Redknapp's passing? Or Stan Collymore's all-round brilliance? Even the eccentricity of James in goal, as he swerved from idiocy to magnificence in the space of one game, was hugely endearing.

And yet there is no place in Premier League history for them or concrete testament to their talent, only fleeting memories of magical moments and the pejorative Spice Boys soubriquet that has stuck with them longer than it ought to have done.

It was not all their fault. John Barnes who, along with Ian Rush, was a survivor of that era's last truly great Liverpool side – the side that had won the old First Division in 1990 – sensed the problem was far more deep-rooted than just the trappings of celebrity glamour. It was a symptom of the club's inability to move with the times, as he explained: 'When I arrived at Liverpool, we had great players and they also bought players with vast experience.

'Training would be yellow bibs versus red bibs, and we were forced to work things out for ourselves. That's fine when you have a whole squad of players with talent and experience, but we were undergoing a transition period under Graeme Souness and all of a sudden, we had a new group that actually needed coaching.

'You can't tell a group just to go out and play, that's where you fall behind the others. We probably didn't help the young players enough. When Roy Evans came in, it was already too late.'

You will never hear a word of criticism for Evans from the group of players he inherited – James, McManaman, Redknapp and Fowler – or those he bought, who included Collymore, Jason McAteer, John Scales and Phil Babb. A 'gentleman' is the most common description, a manager who trusted his players. Perhaps trusted them a little too much.

For a team that had finished sixth and eighth in the first two seasons of the Premier League, too many Liverpool players had the swagger of champions, as if just their presence among football's elite was a passport to the high life.

It is difficult to criticise them because they were all tremendous fun at the time: open, honest, generous in terms of their availability to the media, and all living the kind of life every young man in his twenties would surely have craved. Ultimately, though, they had nothing to show for it other than their bank balances and more headlines in the showbiz columns than on the back pages.

The comparison with Manchester United is invidious. Back-to-back Premier League titles at Old Trafford could have given Fergie's side the right to strut a little, to enjoy life in the spotlight. Instead, so many of that United side were savvy and publicity shy, choosing to let their hair down in a secure environment, well away from celebrity snappers, experienced enough to choose the right time and place for a blow-out.

Gary Neville says, 'The Liverpool lads won't like it, but I've said it before, the reason we won so many leagues in the first few seasons was because of our experienced players. The standards they set on the training pitch, they were so professional. They knew when to have a good time and when not to, and we were taking professionalism to a new level.

'The Liverpool players weren't as professional as us. I don't think they lived their lives as well as us. I don't think they bought into nutrition; the eating, the sports science that had started to develop. They got distracted by things that didn't help them to become better football players.

'They were really good players, talented footballers, and if you had put our manager with them and a couple of our senior players with them, those young lads at Liverpool would have been winning leagues. They were talented young players, but they didn't have the right standard bearers in the dressing room or club.'

Harsh words but a sentiment completely borne out by David James. 'I went to a birthday party at somebody's house and there were a load of the Manchester United players at the party all acting the same way we did when we went out on a Saturday night but in the marquee in this person's garden. I was so annoyed because they were actually doing what we were doing but they were doing it privately, and that was the difference.

'At that time, I think we had a clamour for glamour. Later on in the nineties, David Beckham hit the front pages, but we were trying to do similar things before that. The attention about performance was almost secondary to the attention gained off the field. With the United players, it was, "We are here to win football matches, not appear in this magazine or that magazine."

'If you are highly competitive, you will find something to win. If you are a footballer and your team is winning trophies, that should be sufficient. If you're a footballer and your team is not winning trophies, then getting on the cover of a magazine is a win.'

To this day, Jamie Redknapp bristles at the Spice Boys tag but admits the mentality at Liverpool in the mid nineties left a lot to be desired and also left them wide open to criticism. In the excellent book by Simon Hughes, *Men in White Suits*, Redknapp says, 'There were one or two things Roy [Evans] could have nipped in the bud sooner – things the players couldn't deal with.

'Like when Stan [Collymore] went back to Cannock every day and started missing training sessions. The boys felt like he wasn't pulling his weight and he'd stopped making an effort with people, becoming distant. If Roy had stopped me going down to London every now and then, I would have done exactly as he said, no problem at all. We needed an iron fist a little bit more.'

Without that authority figure at Anfield, the leash on Liverpool players was a long, long one. With Sunday often a day off after a game on Saturday, Liverpool's southern players like Redknapp, Babb and Scales were often accompanied by Jason McAteer and would head for the airport straight from a match and be in London in time for a night out.

While that quartet were enjoying the delights of the capital, Fowler, McManaman, Dominic Matteo and Steve Harkness were more likely to be found closer to home, often accompanied by Spice Girls Emma Bunton, who Fowler dated for a while, and Melanie Chisholm (Sporty Spice never hid her adoration for the club and often wore a Liverpool shirt on stage).

This was the Britpop era, where Cool Britannia ruled and young, good-looking footballers were at the vanguard of the celebrity hedonism that engulfed the whole culture, from politics to music to magazines.

Redknapp had the column in *Smash Hits*, the clothing line and the pop-star girlfriend in Louise from Eternal before Beckham had even clapped eyes on Victoria. In Hughes's book, he says, 'It progressed quicker than anyone could comprehend, when you consider players were having beers and fish and chips on the bus after games just a few years earlier.

'We were focused on what we had to do as professional

football players and what happened on nights out had nothing to do with what happened when we took to the field. I met a pop star; I married a pop star and it added to the whole Spice Boys narrative. People thought image meant more to me and the other lads than football. That was rubbish. Football meant everything to me. I never did anything that would stop me training well, never mind playing well.

'Most of the journalists wanted to talk about the Spice Boys. I became resentful. Maybe that wasn't the right way to deal with things; rather than laugh about it, I got angry. It might have given the wrong impression: that I was too defensive about it. If the papers knew it wound us up, maybe they went for it even more.'

As one of those journalists Redknapp is talking about at the time, I can assure him that it was nothing to do with his attitude. In fact, I can't remember him ever reacting like that. The only ammunition the press needed was being supplied by Liverpool players themselves, like having Robbie Williams on the team bus before a game against Aston Villa in May 1995 – and allowing the pop superstar to accompany them on to the pitch in the build-up.

'Yeah, that typified the difference between Liverpool and Manchester United,' admits James. 'It was quite bizarre, the fact he was allowed on the team bus, this sacred place. I can't imagine Alex Ferguson allowing Gary Barlow on their bus. We all liked Robbie but the fact this pop star was allowed on the bus was not good.

'Chris Evans used to have a television show on a Friday night, and it was during international week and some of our players are on his show and it was just, like, why? It was weird we were more interested in the other stuff than winning games.'

Not that James was immune from indulging in the 'other

stuff', as he puts it. It would lead to the ultimate cross Liverpool players still wear to this day.

Ironically, it could all have been a very different story if Collymore had not cried off sick from a photoshoot for style magazine *Arena Homme+*. Both James and Collymore had been approached by the magazine's picture editor, who asked if they would pose together for a fashion spread, only for Collymore to swerve the shoot, leaving James as the sole model.

Weeks later, his pictures appeared on the front cover and were splashed around the world, catching the eye of Giorgio Armani, who requested James for an advertising campaign to be shot in Seville. Urban myth has it that James asked how much he would be fined if he missed training and, having been told it would be a week's wages, promptly wrote a cheque and told Evans he would see him in a few days. It is a story James categorically denies.

He takes up the story. 'We got to the FA Cup final in 1996 shortly after I did the Armani campaign, and the tradition is you get a cup final suit. I remember walking into the training ground and being told we were getting our suits from Cecil Gee or something like that. Then one of the guys went, 'Jameo, can you get Armani to sort our suits out?'

'And I think, "I don't know Giorgio personally; it's not like I can phone him and ask."' But I knew the guys at Armani so we had a conversation and they agreed to do the suits and said they'd charge us £170, which for an Armani suit is good, but why would the players pay for a suit when we were being offered a perfectly good one for nothing?

'That was it as far as I was concerned. I went to our captain, John Barnes, and said, "Here's the number, deal with Armani."'

What conversations ensued between Barnes and Armani

remain lost in the mists of time. Suffice it to say, to those of us at Wembley who witnessed the Liverpool players walking out of the tunnel for their traditional look at the pitch two hours before kick-off, it is a sight we will never forget.

'They look like fucking ice-cream men,' was the acerbic comment from the late Steve Curry, then chief football writer for the *Daily Express*. And that was one of the kinder verdicts. White suits, pale blue shirts, red-and-white striped ties, blue buttonhole and sunglasses; Liverpool were dressed for a night out in Soho's Emporium nightclub – fitting, really, considering the venue had sponsored the team bus and would be hosting the after-party, win or lose.

'I don't think it was Giorgio that made them,' laughs Redknapp, 'I think it was his brother Billy, because it was the worst suit ever. It was so ill-fitting, it was all over the place, there was no way Giorgio was involved. It was terrible. What we should have done is just said, "No, we're not wearing that." It was a massive mistake from our point of view; we should have just worn our club suit that was blue or black.'

To be fair, the suits were no crime against fashion and the twenty-nine-year-old me was eaten up with envy that the Liverpool boys could pull it off so supremely. It was just the fact it yet again gave people such a brutal stick with which to beat them. Manchester United – inevitably their cup final opponents – winning the Double would undoubtedly have been the best story on the day from a journalistic perspective, but I recall praying Liverpool would pull it off, just to protect some decent people from the flak defeat would bring.

It was not to be. A hugely disappointing final was settled when James flapped at a Beckham corner five minutes from the end, it glanced off Ian Rush's chest before Eric Cantona volleyed past a gaggle of Liverpool players for the winning goal. In later years, Ferguson would claim he used the sight of the suits as a psychological tool with which to rev up his side, calling them 'ridiculous' and the decision to wear them as 'arrogant and over-confident'.

'For Alex Ferguson to say that he knew United had won when he saw us before the game is absolute rubbish,' claims Redknapp. 'There was nothing in the game, it was a terrible game, just a moment of brilliance from Cantona defined it. Had we won the cup that year, I honestly think we'd have gone on and dominated for a long time, like United did.

'It was a pivotal couple of weeks because it was the first time the Nevilles, Beckham, Nicky Butt and Paul Scholes experienced success with the first team. They got the taste for it and carried on; it gave them the confidence to grow. We had the potential to be a really great side too, but we never experienced that taste. We needed the experience of beating one of our rivals to a trophy, but it never happened.'

Would that particular group of Liverpool players have been able to handle the kind of pressure success inevitably brings? James is unsure. 'We would have been the best-dressed team to ever win the FA Cup and it would have probably helped catapult us. It might have sent us into outer space, and we wouldn't have been able to control it.

'Because we lost, because we were dressed like a band, there was no positive spin. We could have been on the same trajectory as United and that was the pivotal point. That's the point where, from a Liverpool point of view, the Premier League was written off.'

There would be improvements in the league over the next two seasons as Liverpool finished fourth and then third, but final positions could not disguise the gulf between themselves and both United and Arsenal. Lessons had been learned off the pitch, the sobering experience of Wembley ridicule enough to convince many of the players that life in the limelight had its darker side. But on the pitch, they were continually in the shade as far as the Premier League was concerned.

When Gerard Houllier arrived at Anfield – initially to partner Evans and then replace him – those who had craved professionalism fell victim to the new regime. Collymore went before Houllier's arrival, while Redknapp, Fowler and James never fully convinced the Frenchman of their worth and were forced to find pastures new. With McManaman leaving for Real Madrid on a free transfer, Liverpool were building around the youth of Michael Owen, Steven Gerrard and Jamie Carragher, players who would remain the cornerstone of Anfield for years to come.

So, regrets over a career squandered? Not for Redknapp. 'Being a footballer first and foremost was my passion, that was my love. You think, "How different would it be to play now?" But there's much more intrusion with camera phones and all that. When I was playing, it was an amazing time to be a footballer; you had the best of fun, it was a great time. I look back and think it was probably the most exciting time to be a footballer because there wasn't the pressure the players are under now. You could enjoy it a lot more than the players do now.

'Yes, the Spice Boys thing does wind me up still, but I'd have been a bit disappointed if I'd have been the Spice Girls because they were a huge success, a lot bigger success than we were ...'

13

Crazy Gang, Crazy Plan

A football club never truly loses its soul. It can be threatened by imposters and have its roots ripped out but still it survives, a flickering remnant of life protected by those who love and nurture it, even in its darkest days.

Take a walk down Plough Lane and you come across a housing development bearing the names of Wimbledon heroes: Bassett House, Cork House, Lawrie (Sanchez) House, even one named after the last chairman of what I consider the true football club, Stanley Reed. Stroll a little further and you come across the Cherry Red Records Stadium, built on the site of the old greyhound stadium but only a Dave Beasant clearance from where the old ground once stood.

It is the heart of a thriving club, AFC Wimbledon, back in its spiritual home in the London borough, built from the ashes of the despicable move to Milton Keynes and driven by supporters who have constantly fought attempts to kill it off.

I have to declare an interest here. I was the local reporter covering Wimbledon for the *South London Press* from the year the club won the FA Cup in 1988 until 1992, when Plough Lane was my second home. Its ramshackle facilities were despised by so many journalists who were forced into a press box that amounted to little more than a concrete bench, covered by a leaking roof and with windows that steamed up the moment it was full.

But I loved the fact the club was open and lacking in pretension, that the players' lounge was basically a nightclub called Nelsons and fans mingled with their heroes after a game, buying them pints, chatting about the match. I loved the training ground right on the A3 out of London, where breakfast was a bacon and egg sandwich and a cup of tea in a transport café alongside lorry drivers and cabbies who shared the facilities with Vinnie Jones, Dennis Wise and John Fashanu.

More than anything, I adored the indomitable spirit of a club that continually punched above its weight (and I use the term in every sense of the word) but suffered not the slightest illusion of grandeur, having battled its way up from non-league to the old First Division, literally bloodying noses along the way, fighting for acceptance before establishing itself among the elite.

You had to be tough to survive among them. The true architects of the Crazy Gang, Steve Galliers and Wally Downes, were either gone or peripheral figures, but the mentality persisted. Step out of line and you knew that a price would have to be paid, like the moment Jones held me by the throat in the first-team dressing room following something I had written in the match-day programme. Or when Fashanu took particular umbrage at the fact I had identified him as the Wimbledon player spoken to by police after a tunnel brawl with Manchester United.

As so many supposedly better teams found to their cost, take a backwards step against Wimbledon and they would hunt you down. As owner Sam Hammam said on their arrival in the First Division, 'We have to remain the British Bulldog, SAS club. We have to sustain ourselves with sheer power and the attitude that we will kick ass. Before we go down, we'll have a stream of blood from here to Timbuktu.'

Fighting words. Hammam revelled in that kind of imagery, the underdog against the world, upsetting their gentrified neighbours with a combination of streetwise devilment and football savvy. How perverse, then, that it should he Hammam who did so much to threaten the club's existence with a series of decisions that began the inexorable move towards Milton Keynes.

The first decision was painful yet understandable. Plough Lane, for all its idiosyncrasies, was no longer fit for purpose in a post-Hillsborough world. The demands of the Taylor Report meant a future at the old ground was unsustainable. The expense of making it all-seater would financially cripple the Dons and so the move seven miles across South London to Selhurst Park in 1991 for a groundshare with Crystal Palace at least made some kind of sense.

For four years, Wimbledon fans were sustained by the promise of a return to Merton at some stage and fought their own battles with Merton Council when it seemed those dreams were being stymied by politicians and bureaucracy. Those same supporters believed that everybody within the club was committed to the cause and that a dreary life at Selhurst was just a temporary displacement, something that could be tolerated in the short term.

Hammam, though, was plotting a very different course, one that extended way beyond the boundaries of South London. For some years, Hammam's public and private views on where Wimbledon should play its football were diametrically opposed. In front of the fans, he talked about a return to its Merton roots and how politicians must never be allowed to scupper this vision.

But bellicose demands gave way to more devious plotting

behind closed doors. Word reached me that Hammam and a series of property developers had tentatively looked at sites as far away as Gatwick and Basingstoke as potential new homes for the Dons. While these plans never got even as close as the blueprint stage, it was clear Hammam had set his sights further afield than South London.

Nobody seems to know exactly when Dublin came on to the horizon, although from the moment Joe Kinnear took over as manager in early 1992, the link was there. For all his London 'geezer' attitude, Kinnear had been born in Dublin and won twenty-six Republic of Ireland caps during his time as a cultured full-back for Spurs and he kept close contacts across the Irish Sea.

I liked Joe but I could never once trust him, given that he seemed either to forget half the lies he told you or to convince himself they were true. He also had the worst 'tell' when he was spinning you a line: his gaze would wander somewhere over your right shoulder into the middle distance, and he would scratch his head behind his right ear with his middle finger. Working with him on a daily basis was fun but also a tortuous experience, as you tried to distil fact from outright fabrication when it came to team news or transfers.

Whether Kinnear ever believed there was a serious chance an English football club could simply up sticks and transport itself to another country, I cannot be sure. One day he would seem utterly sincere in the veracity of this seemingly preposterous proposal, the next he would confess he was only going along with it to pacify Hammam. What is clear is that he was a prime mover at the initial stages once Hammam saw an opportunity in Dublin.

In 1994, Kinnear reached out to Eamon Dunphy, former player turned author, journalist and pundit, with whom he had shared a dressing room on international duty. Dunphy

was the perfect fit for such a maverick plan; a disruptor long
before the term gained such significance in business, Dunphy
used his status as one of Ireland's football voices to lambast
what he saw as the parochialism of the game in his country,
with the League of Ireland and the Football Association of
Ireland (the FAI) as perennial targets for his ire.

Energised at the thought of possibly making such an
impactful statement as bringing a Premier League club to
Ireland, Dunphy quickly put together a consortium that
included U2's manager, Paul McGuinness, as well as the head
of Ticketmaster and a director of HMV in Ireland, Owen
O'Callaghan.

Dunphy said, 'I thought it was a great idea, I thought
it was very doable because I thought Dublin could host a
Premier League club and do so a lot more successfully than
Wimbledon in South London. Owen O'Callaghan had a
stadium site with planning permission, so I met him and he
was very excited about it and very proactive. He became the
leading figure on our side of the project.'

It did not generally take much to motivate Hammam, just
tell him his plan was ridiculous and unworkable and all his
energy would be devoted to proving you wrong. For eighteen
months, he worked tirelessly behind the scenes to build a business plan and explore the logistics behind a potential move.
Crucially, he sounded out a number of fellow Premier League
chairmen who, while not exactly enthusiastic, could see the
benefits of a new audience in Dublin where, traditionally,
interest in English football dwarfed the League of Ireland.
The Premier League, however, refused to state any position,
although now, talking to those involved at the time, they were
secure in the belief that both FIFA and UEFA statutes would
prevent the move.

It gave Hammam the confidence to go public and in 1996

he travelled to Dublin to meet some of the city's most influential journalists in a bid to convince them of the merits of his scheme. Alongside Dunphy, he also recruited a lawyer, Jean-Louis Dupont, who, a few years earlier, had won a landmark case representing Jean-Marc Bosman, which led to complete freedom of movement for players at the end of their contracts. If the authorities wanted a fight, Hammam figured, why not recruit a man capable of landing punches? It was a typical Wimbledon tactic.

Another, which Hammam had mastered, was to pronounce loudly and aggressively at every opportunity. How could anybody stand in the way of such a visionary plan? Who was going to prevent Wimbledon from becoming a powerhouse in Dublin? Why would anybody want to deny the people of Ireland an outlet to satisfy their fanaticism for the game?

Suddenly, airy proposals became 'facts'. Wimbledon, buoyed by an influx of Sky television money and increased sponsorship, would pay each League of Ireland club £250,000 as a 'golden hello', as well as funding infrastructure for club academies. Wimbledon fans would, apparently, be flown to Dublin home games for free, courtesy of Ryanair, while Hammam would implement security measures around the stadium to ensure there was no repeat of the rioting that had marred England's visit to Lansdowne Road a year earlier. These were heady times for Hammam, and he was not about to be derailed by piffling matters such as competition integrity, the existential threat to the League of Ireland or FIFA's regulations that precluded clubs from playing across international borders. 'Talk loudly and carry a big stick' could have been Hammam's motto.

Dunphy and Kinnear were swept along with the whole concept of the 'Dublin Dons', Dunphy proclaiming, 'Ireland has the opportunity to be a first world football country', while

Kinnear claimed that he had turned down huge managerial jobs in favour of leading Wimbledon towards the promised land of his birth. What those jobs were, nobody could actually pin down, although Kinnear let it be known that Celtic, Spurs and Manchester City had all, apparently, been rebuffed.

Wimbledon's traditional fan base was not only the smallest in the Premier League, but it was also dwarfed by many clubs in the lower leagues. Yet while small in number, they were loud of voice. There may have been admiration for what Hammam had achieved as chairman and affection for his gregarious nature, but there was also suspicion that led directly back to his half-hearted plans to merge with Palace in 1987. Now suspicion was replaced with outright contempt.

That anger was matched in Ireland by every League of Ireland club and their fans who, quite rightly, foresaw a Premier League powerhouse arriving on their shores and swallowing up sponsorship opportunities and commercial deals without a thought for the native game. It was that threat which mobilised the FAI.

It became clear very quickly that Hammam and, to an extent, Kinnear had underestimated the passion of the anti-Dublin supporters. The more the pair cosied up to the Irish media with a series of off-the-record dinners and on-the-record interviews, the more it antagonised the fans both at home and in Ireland. 'Dublin = Death' banners and leaflets became commonplace at Wimbledon matches home and away.

One of the major mistakes Hammam made was basing his arguments for the move on purely commercial grounds. He had been an early convert to the idea of the Premier League five years before, understanding that a huge boost in broadcast rights would help make up for the shortfall sparse crowds at Plough Lane created. Sky's money was helping to keep Wimbledon competitive and average crowds at Selhurst were rising by around two thousand annually. It was difficult for Hammam to seriously point to an economic decline in the club's future.

The more he banged on about the need to balance the books, the more the fans reacted with disgust that their club was being ripped from them and hawked overseas. It was cold-hearted business pragmatism against the raw emotion of losing a football club from the community in which it had been nurtured. Dunphy made the same mistake in Ireland, trumpeting the trickle-down benefits of Premier League football while being drowned out by supporters who prophesied the death of the National League within a very short space of time. Dunphy's argument that the presence of Manchester United in Lancashire did not threaten the likes of Rochdale, Oldham and Bury now, in hindsight, appears fatally flawed.

Traditionally, any fan protest has needed a champion in high places or a position of power. Fortunately for the anti-Dublin brigade, they found somebody who ticked both those boxes. While the Premier League opted to hide behind UEFA and FIFA regulations which appeared to preclude a team based in a country outside the UK competing in its leagues, FAI chief executive Bernard O'Byrne was happy to be front and centre of the denunciation of Hammam's plans.

O'Byrne fought ferociously to protect the FAI's position, writing to the Premier League in the strongest terms, describing Hammam's financial offers as 'Judas money' and rallying behind a cause which had seen over three hundred Irish fans gather in a Dublin hotel in September 1996 to coordinate their own fight and protests. He told the *Daily Mirror*, 'The motivations are the sort of greed that is enveloping football everywhere right now.'

Still Hammam fought on, having convinced himself his fight was just, that he was battling to preserve the lifeblood of his football club. Well, at least until an alternative reared its head.

By the time the twenty-two League of Ireland clubs voted unanimously against the move in 1997, Hammam was exploring fresh opportunities. Those who knew him best among the fan base were surprised at the magnanimous way he accepted the decision without all the threats and accusations and suspected something else was afoot.

Those suspicions were confirmed when Hammam sold 80 per cent of his shares in the club to Norwegian businessmen Bjørn Rune Gjelsten and Kjell Inge Røkke, and while Dublin remained on the horizon, there was little impetus to continue the fight. By the summer of 1998 it was quietly forgotten.

For Dunphy and his Irish consortium, the thought occurred that they had been masterfully played by Hammam. As Dunphy admitted: 'I spent three years on it, which turned out to be a terrible waste of time. The problem person was Hammam, to some extent. We weren't sure how genuine his offer was.

'The whole thing tailed off when he found a couple of Norwegian shipping magnates and he sold Wimbledon to them. In the back of his mind, he was looking for us to get someone else, we were the sprat to catch a mackerel.'

Within two years of the 'Dublin Dons' being dead in the water, Hammam had sold the last of his shares to the Norwegians and had moved on to another country and another fight, taking over at Cardiff City and promising to make them the only team in Wales fans should follow. It was textbook Hammam: long on rhetoric if somewhat short on logic.

The Wimbledon I loved remained homeless at Selhurst Park and while they still had the ability to spring the odd surprise, something had been lost. Kinnear was temporarily forced out of the game at the end of the 1998–99 season after suffering a heart attack before a game at Sheffield Wednesday. Hammam appointed Norwegian Egil Olsen, whose main claim to fame in a short-lived stint was that he turned up for pre-season training in wellies.

Worse was to come. The club's finances were shambolic, the players failed to respond to Olsen, and with two games to go and relegation looking inevitable, he was sacked and replaced by Terry Burton, who had been part of the Wimbledon story for twelve years but had no heroic final chapter to add.

To be frank, I lost interest in Wimbledon around this time as the club I once covered and loved grew even more faceless, devoid of character and lacking the warmth that had been its defining feature. When news began to filter out that the Norwegian owners were considering a move to Milton Keynes, I could not pretend I was shocked, it was just an endgame from people who knew their way around a balance sheet and not much more.

But the spirit that had empowered the fight against the move to Dublin still burnt within the support base. Franchise FC could crawl their way up the M1; the real Wimbledon would always survive as the fans and those loyal to what remained of the club turned their backs on MK Dons and were given resurrection in the form of AFC Wimbledon. Now this was something I could get behind, even from a distance.

Through it all, the words of Marc Jones came back vividly. Marc was one of those fans who had led the fight against the move to Ireland and who had vowed that, if it came to fruition, he would help form a non-league club. As he explained, 'The Dublin thing proved to us as Wimbledon fans that it isn't about whether you win the Premier League or the FA Cup. It isn't about how many people are watching you, it isn't about how good your centre forward is and how much money you've got in the transfer market.

'What makes a football club is the area it's born from, the area that it represents. And if you take that away, it's not football any more. It's baseball then, it's American football, it's just a bullshit sport.'

14

Fury to Fantasy

Anger. It was the defining emotion of the greatest season the English game has witnessed. In the manager's office, at the training ground, in the boardroom, on the terraces; in 1998, Old Trafford was seething.

It started at the top, even above the head of Alex Ferguson. Rattled at having been beaten to the title by Arsenal, there was also a growing feeling that Ferguson had taken his eye off the ball, that the arrival of Arsène Wenger had exposed a weakness in the Scot and that Manchester United were now falling behind in terms of recruitment, sports science and even motivation.

Ferguson himself had sensed the drop-off during the previous season when United threw away an eleven-point lead over Arsenal at the turn of the year and were desperately flagging by the time Wenger's side won ten Premier League games in a row. He hinted darkly at changes, telling *The Times*, 'People like myself and the staff and the supporters do not deserve to have everything thrown away by the players like this, not after all the work that has been done here.

'The club is like a moving bus; we're not waiting at the stop for anyone who is late and I've always made that point to players. We have to make sure the bus goes on now, we cannot stop.'

Yet for the club chairman, Martin Edwards, and the chairman of United's PLC board, Roland Smith, the players were not solely to blame, no matter how much Ferguson protested otherwise. The manager wanted to strengthen the squad with signings, most notably Patrick Kluivert from AC Milan or Aston Villa's Dwight Yorke to bolster the attack, while he had already made the first moves to sign Dutch defender Jaap Stam.

Edwards baulked at the expenditure, pointing out that Ferguson's last six recommendations – Teddy Sheringham, Ronny Johnsen, Ole Gunnar Solskjaer, Jordi Cruyff, Henning Berg and Karel Poborsky – were hardly setting Old Trafford alight and that perhaps other people's judgement might play more of a part in recruitment.

It set the stage for a combustible confrontation when Ferguson was summoned back from his beloved South of France to face Edwards and Smith at a meeting in Central London. Over an hour of talks that swerved between the barely polite and the outright contemptuous, Ferguson was faced with the kind of criticism and scrutiny he had not experienced since the dark days of 'Ta ra Fergie'.

If Edwards had any doubts over the strategy of antagonising his manager, he does not appear to have any regrets, as he pointed out almost a decade later: 'At the time, we felt we just slipped a bit, having done the Double two years before. We hadn't won anything and, to be honest, we were dissatisfied. We wondered if Alex had taken his eye off the ball a little. So we told him our feelings and Roland thought we should follow it up with a letter. We called Alex back from holiday. He wasn't pleased; it didn't go down that well. He received the letter and came pretty much straight back in to see me.

He was furious, saying: "If that's what you think of me then get stuffed ... I am resigning." And off he went. I can't say I was particularly concerned as I thought he would come back. Happily I was right. These things happen in business and football clubs but as long as you come out the right side, it's justifiable.'

Justifiable or not, Ferguson was ablaze after such a searching examination of his managerial credentials. But if he was waiting for Edwards to back down, he was mistaken and, faced with the prospect of a future without Manchester United, decided discretion may well be the better part of valour: he asked Edwards to ignore his resignation.

Was it a deliberate ploy, to spark something in Ferguson that may have been missing in the 1997–8 campaign? Edwards is non-committal, adding only, 'We always supported Alex and he is not a man to bear grudges, but the combination of him refocusing plus the new players saw us kick on again.'

Suddenly, for Ferguson, there were enemies to confront – just the way he liked it. Wenger was an obvious foe and now his own board had ganged up against him, it played perfectly into what psychologist Bill Beswick described as Ferguson's 'fighter mentality'.

Beswick had been recommended to Ferguson after his work with high-performance athletes, including the England basketball team and several American college teams. It was part of a longer-term transformation behind the scenes at Old Trafford that Ferguson immediately recognised as necessary.

Beswick says, 'Alex was smart, he knew how to adapt. The game was changing rapidly and Manchester United were not immune to that, and although it's a big, powerful club, keeping it at the top of the tree was a real task, so he had to amend his philosophy. The first time I met him, he said, "Bill, how do I keep my team number one?" I said, "Alex, every day, think, train and behave like you're number two." And he went to his desk and wrote that down.

'He had to fight for everything he ever got. There's two mentalities, fighter and victim, and most people sway between the two. Very few are completely fighter or completely victim, but Alex was one of those that locked into fighter mentality, he couldn't ever find a reason to be a victim. He always fought back, that was his magnificent strength, and he was a wonderful person to be around because he was unshakable.'

The same warrior ethos that had galvanised Ferguson also ran through Roy Keane, almost to the point of resentment. He had been missing for most of the previous campaign after rupturing his cruciate ligaments and partly blamed himself for United relinquishing their Premier League crown to an Arsenal side Keane identified as the greatest threat he had faced.

Always driven, now there was a mania about Keane's dedication to the United cause. He arrived back for pre-season having shed weight and with a shaven skull, an appearance that now more than matched his fearsome desire never to take a backward step. From the moment Keane threw himself into a tackle on Patrick Vieira during the Charity Shield at Wembley a week before the league season began, it was clear he was prepared for the battle ahead.

But even with Ferguson and Keane fully focused, the anger among the United faithful could not be so easily diluted, not when they believed the very soul of their football club was at stake.

In June, Edwards had found himself at Sky's studios near Heathrow Airport, ostensibly to discuss the channel's plans for a pay-per-view option in the Premier League. Instead, Edwards found himself ambushed with the news that Rupert Murdoch wanted to buy United and was willing to pay a premium for the shares, a premium that looked likely to net Edwards in the region of £80 million for his own shares.

For almost three months, Edwards kept the news from everybody outside a tight group of United directors, both at club and PLC level. This *omertà* was designed to keep the news of Murdoch's offer away from Ferguson for fear a loose word in the wrong ear from the manager would jeopardise the whole deal. It was another mistake that would further serve to alienate Ferguson.

He discovered the truth in September when a brilliant scoop in the *Sunday Telegraph* trumpeted the news Murdoch had launched a £575 million bid and that the majority of the United board were in favour of selling. It left Ferguson isolated. Instinctively, he sensed it was wrong and that the supporters would rebel, but he also knew that to say anything would mobilise the fan base against the board and potentially destabilise the club as a whole.

Ferguson need not have worried, the fans were capable of righteous indignation without any prompting from him, and there was an immediate uprising against Murdoch, Edwards and anybody within the club who appeared in even the slightest favour of the deal.

They found an ally in, of all people, Greg Dyke. The man who had helped drive the formation of the Premier League, only to be jettisoned when Murdoch waved a much bigger cheque under the noses of twenty-two club chairmen for broadcast rights, found himself in a position to strike a retaliatory blow. He was now an independent director at Old Trafford and railed against what he saw as Murdoch's potentially unhealthy presence on both the television and the club side of the play. Like Ferguson, his instincts were sound.

But even Dyke at his most dogged found himself virtually a lone voice when Murdoch resorted to his usual tactic of simply raising the financial stakes, and when the share offer made to United valued the club at £623 million, Dyke, with much reluctance, agreed to the sale.

If the board had acquiesced, then the fans were not about to be so easily bought. They rallied, they found the loudest of militant voices, they organised themselves into a unified and compelling opposition and they took the fight to both United and Sky. They also won a significant victory when Mark Booth, the American chief executive of BSkyB and the man fronting Murdoch's bid, failed to identify United's left back when put on the spot by a reporter from the *Daily Mirror*, leaving himself – and the bid – open to widespread ridicule.

It was against the backdrop of this fomenting rage from all quarters that Ferguson gathered his troops. 'Sir Alex saw football as a duel,' Gary Neville recalls. 'You know he couldn't be seen to back down against an opposition manager who was trying to take him on, he was never going to do that. If someone was going against him, he would stand up to that challenge, it wouldn't bother him a bit. He was so blinkered; Manchester United winning was the only thing that mattered.

'I think he thrived on the challenge, the angst and the tension that existed between top teams, and he felt he would always come out top in those battles. When your manager is going out there, taking on the opposition manager, where does that leave his players? They've got to be behind him because he's not changing.'

Ferguson had at least been partially successful in his battle with Edwards over transfer targets. He missed out on Kluivert, who opted for Barcelona over Manchester, but landed Yorke, Stam and Jesper Blomqvist from Parma, an outlay of £26 million that at last began to make a statement in the market that had been missing for the last few years.

Not that fresh blood in the squad seemed capable of

WORLD BEATERS: Juninho was at the peak of his powers when he joined Middlesbrough in 1995 while Ruud Gullit and Gianluca Vialli were Chelsea's princes of the King's Road

PERFECTION?: No other side in the Premier League era
has matched Arsenal's unbeaten campaign of 2003–04

changing the pattern of the previous season. David Beckham's first goal since the torrid events of the World Cup was just about the only bright spot of the opening five games, which saw United end September in fifth place, having also lost 3–0 to Arsenal at Highbury.

In truth, for all Ferguson's tactical savvy and experience, he was unable to make United tick. It was almost as if there was too much talent at his disposal in attack to come up with a cohesive plan. Yorke was partnered with Teddy Sheringham, Andy Cole, Solskjaer and even Ryan Giggs, as Ferguson sought some kind of solution, but it was not until October, when Yorke and Cole sparked into life against Southampton, that the manager sensed that was his duo of choice.

Off the pitch, it was not exactly sweetness and light in the United dressing room. Keane and Sheringham, who had hardly been bosom buddies during their days together at Nottingham Forest, were now not speaking to each other. Sheringham was also using Yorke as a go-between in his relationship with Cole after the pair had fallen out on England duty four years before. And still results in the Premier League failed to set the pulses racing.

Thankfully, there was the distraction of Europe and the Champions League. Finishing second behind Arsenal meant United had to qualify for the group stages, something that was comfortably achieved against the Polish side Lodz, even if it meant a competitive game before the domestic season had kicked off. With Lodz dispatched, United went into the toughest quartet of the group stages alongside Barcelona, Bayern Munich and Brondby.

The pleasure Ferguson took from draws home and away both in Spain and Germany was tempered by United's relative mediocrity in the Premier League. As thrilling as two 3–3 draws were with Barcelona, Ferguson was beginning to suspect his team were a big-game side, more enraptured by the challenge of great European encounters than the bread and butter of the League.

Things reached a head in November when United went to Sheffield Wednesday and were outplayed in the first half. Ferguson often claims his reputation for dressing-room tirades is overstated and that they were used far more sparingly than legend suggests. At Hillsborough that afternoon, nobody was spared. Even those players who had been alongside him for several years admit to never having witnessed fury like it: a decimation of United's apathetic approach to the game and the domestic season as a whole, singling out individuals for ferocious criticism, going around the whole team with accusations that were painful to hear for some, inspiring for others.

That 3–1 defeat was not quite the turning point it might have been. However, it was a bloodletting of sorts that allowed even the strongest characters to reassess where they stood within the club, the most notable being Peter Schmeichel.

The goalkeeper had been playing as late as 3 July when Denmark went out of the 1998 World Cup against Brazil and had had just ten days off through the summer, his return hastened by the need to play that Champions League qualifying round. As stoic as he sometimes might have appeared, he was suffering – and for the first time admitted it.

'Perhaps I should have consulted someone about it,' Schmeichel now concedes, 'but I was absolutely flying, I was playing so well and so fit from the World Cup, and then I hit the wall, absolutely hit the wall.

'I played awfully in the Wednesday game. I made a very big mistake, and the media were all picking up on it, so I actually ended up knocking on Fergie's door, saying sorry for my performance but just that I was so tired, completely drained. I needed to get away.'

It was a situation made for Ferguson as he looked into the face of a player who had served him so well but was now desperate for help. He challenged Schmeichel: get United through Christmas and then, in the New Year, take ten days off with the family, disappear to a beach or wherever you want. 'I came away thinking, "Wow." Just thinking about it made me fresher.

'This was going to be my last season and he said to make sure it was a good one because he thought there was something special happening.'

Speak now to United players and, more than two decades later, they can tick off moments in the Premier League season where the tide began to turn their way, or a small but significant moment altered the whole mindset. One of those was a 3–2 defeat at home to Middlesbrough when Ferguson was on compassionate leave, one of only four matches he missed in his entire time at Old Trafford.

Again, there was a post-mortem at the training ground but led by the players themselves. Again, nobody emerged unscathed. It is an indication of the strength of the group that weaknesses and failings could be exposed but there was neither fracture nor ramifications within the squad.

As Arsenal had discovered the previous season, perhaps a club has to stare into the abyss.

Before the Middlesbrough game, Brian Kidd had left United to take up the manager's role at Blackburn Rovers. It was a move that had been on the cards since the summer after Ferguson discovered his assistant had been discussing transfer targets with the board, behaviour the manager saw as tantamount to betrayal. In his place, Ferguson recruited Steve McClaren from Derby, having been impressed with a game plan the coach had devised to stifle David Beckham the season before. McClaren brought fresh eyes and a fresh perspective. He also brought Bill Beswick with him.

Roy Keane was always suspicious of new faces at the club, be they players or coaches, and they had to be tested before receiving his reluctant seal of approval. While remaining diffident to Beswick on the surface, Keane was intrigued enough to find out more about the methodology, he just did not want anybody knowing about it.

Smart enough to realise his injury of the previous season meant a lifestyle change as well, Keane had given up drinking and late-night revelry – his 'Irish weekends', as Ferguson cuttingly described them. Stripping back to around a mere five per cent body fat had given the United captain a physical advantage in his fights against Vieira and the rest; now he sought a mental lift.

'He came to see me,' Beswick recalls. 'He walked up behind me, came really close and said, "I need to see you."

'"I know you do, come and talk to me."

'"No, I don't want the other players to see."

'"Well, I'm telling you, you've got a real problem."

'"I know. Can I meet you this afternoon at two thirty? McDonald's. A50."

'So, I had to go to McDonald's on the A50 so no other player would see him talking to me!'

As complex as Keane may have been as a character, his defining motivation was easy for Beswick to identify. 'I spoke to the players about the evolution of the player through various stages, but with the ultimate stage being the warrior athlete, and that really rang bells with Roy.

'We worked a lot together, shared a lot of ideas, and he was a very interesting guy. Not easy, but fascinating, and I grew to respect him an awful lot. When I got there, Roy was a classic warrior athlete. For example, I understood why Roy hated friendly games: you don't put a warrior out to fight when there's no meaning, he has to have a dragon to slay.

'Arsenal were terrific for him because they provided a dragon and that's what Roy needed; he needed a consistent challenge, and the warrior athlete is someone who goes beyond what most athletes would do in order to win.

'The difficulty with being a warrior athlete is that you are an extraordinary athlete, but you remain at essence an ordinary person. And it's switching between those two roles. So, you're an ordinary person driving to the training ground, stopping at red lights like the rest of us do, but when you get to training, you've got to switch persona and become the warrior athlete, the performer. But then going back out from the club, back into your car, going home to your wife and kids, you have to switch back to the ordinary person, be ready to go to the supermarket and help with the shopping, hold the baby, whatever happens.

'And those transition moments from ordinary person to extraordinary athlete are not easy unless somebody helps them with it.'

If Middlesbrough was the catalyst and Keane the ultimate leader, it was Yorke who provided the mantra for the remainder of the season. Off the back of the training-ground showdown between the players, Yorke had gone through the fixtures and worked out that all United had to do was avoid defeat in the next thirty-three games and they would win the lot, the unprecedented Treble that, before then, had not even been whispered.

And as each game went by, it would be Yorke's grin that reminded the rest it was only thirty-two, thirty-one, thirty . . . inexorably moving closer towards history.

The New Year saw United gather the kind of momentum

that would ultimately prove unstoppable, even if it did need a little dose of fabled 'Fergie time' to help them out. Revenge against Middlesbrough in the third round of the FA Cup saw United drawn at home to Liverpool. Trailing to a Michael Owen goal, it looked as if Yorke's countdown was at an end until, with two minutes left to play, he scored the equaliser and watched as Solskjaer hit a shot through Jamie Carragher's legs to win it with seconds to go. An omen?

In the League, United's reputation for never knowing when they were beaten was reaching epic status, as Gary Neville recalls: 'Every big game that season was special, we seemed to win every single game in the last few minutes and it epitomised what Sir Alex was; that never say die, never give in, go to the very end with the determination and will to win.

'Whether it was Liverpool in the cup, coming from behind against Tottenham in the final Premier League game of the season, to the Champions League final, it just felt like what Manchester United should be as a football club – enthralling, exciting, magic, taking risks, playing attacking football.

'Throw everything in the box in the final five minutes, even if you're 2–0 down. You might lose 4–0 but you might win 3–2.'

Six against Leicester City, eight against Nottingham Forest, with Solskjaer scoring four times in less than fourteen minutes from the bench, this was free-wheeling fantasy football for the fans, as match after match was ticked off without defeat.

Fulham and then Chelsea in the FA Cup both fell, Internazionale were comfortably beaten in Europe, and suddenly United were top of the Premier League and in two other semi-finals. For Schmeichel, even after everything he had achieved at the club, it was a ride he will never forget: 'It was the most fun moment in my life as a footballer.

'It was so hard. I had a groin injury, I could hardly kick

a ball and every game I had to dig so deep just to get on the pitch, but I loved it, absolutely loved it. The stakes were so high and every little thing you did carried an impact and I was so tired all the time, I could hardly drive my car, that's how tired I was. It was a completely crazy period, the last fourteen games we only had 3.8 days between each one and every single game was the same as playing a cup final.'

In the midst of this adrenalin high came the news the supporters craved as much as even results on the pitch. Just days before the FA Cup semi-final with Arsenal, on 11 April, the Government's Mergers and Monopolies Commission blocked the proposed Murdoch takeover and the fight against BSkyB was won. It may not have been on Yorke's countdown list, but it was a victory as significant as any that year.

The fourteen days between 7 and 21 April 1999 saw Manchester United involved in four of the most enthralling games of their history. Even now, twenty-three years later, it defies belief at the way they came through them.

7 APRIL: Only a Ryan Giggs goal two minutes into injury time rescued a draw for United against Juventus in the first leg of the Champions League semi-final. They would now need to go to Turin and either win or clinch a score draw of 2–2 or higher to reach their first final since 1968.

11 APRIL: A gripping FA Cup semi-final at Aston Villa saw neither United nor Arsenal able to find the winner, although Keane had what looked like a perfectly good goal chalked off for a controversial offside against Yorke.

14 APRIL: A game for the ages and possibly the finest semi-final the old competition has ever witnessed. Beckham's long-range effort gave United the lead only for Dennis Bergkamp to equalise after a shot flicked past Schmeichel off Stam. Keane, the ultimate warrior, received a red card for fouls on Bergkamp and Marc Overmars before Phil

Neville pulled down Freddie Ljungberg in the box. Somehow, Schmeichel flung himself to his left to parry away Bergkamp's penalty. Enter Giggs, a blur of pace and perfect balance to fire high past David Seaman.

21 APRIL: What unfurled in the Stadio Delle Alpi was simply one of the greatest performances in United's history. Two down after just eleven minutes, even Ferguson believed the dream was over. He had reckoned without Keane. The captain pulled one back and betrayed not a flicker of emotion and only a sharp rebuke to Blomqvist when his ball sold Keane short and his foul on Zinedine Zidane meant he would miss the final. Not that it affected Keane one iota, he simply kept driving United forward.

Cole and Yorke combined for an equaliser which replenished United's soul and then it was just two great clubs, two great fighters, throwing everything they had at each other until both were out on their feet, time only for Yorke to dance through before being tripped and Cole picking up the loose ball for the most memorable of victories.

Now we are into single figures. While Arsenal fought to stay in touch in the League, the wave of euphoria carrying United forward grew stronger and more powerful until all it needed was a victory against Spurs on the final day of the Premier League season. Of course, they fell behind, why would they do it the easy way? Goals from Beckham and Cole either side of half-time were inevitable and the title was United's.

Less than a week later, Newcastle United were swept aside at Wembley in an FA Cup victory so comfortable I had written my match report by around seventy-five minutes, with only the window dressing of the trophy lift to add on at the final whistle.

Strangely, the Double, normally a superlative achievement, felt anti-climactic, a mere stepping-stone towards something greater, something truly historic . . .

Books have been written about that night in the Nou Camp on 26 May 1999 where chaos and delirium were the only emotions; where Manchester United – belligerent, brilliant Manchester United – created a tableau never witnessed before in the English game.

It could happen again, of course, although the chances of it being United are disappearing with every season that passes. Ferguson built more great teams but none with that same essence of character, that ability to almost torture themselves in the depths they had to search within. Man for man, I am not sure they stand up to the scrutiny of comparison with Ronaldo, Rooney, Tevez, Ferdinand and Vidić, but as a collective, I would take the 1999 team over every other side that followed.

And Ferguson? Well, the only thing that soured the season for him was David Ginola being voted the Football Writers' Association Footballer of the Year. In our defence, so many United players won votes that they actually split the overall vote, allowing Ginola to win 'for one fucking goal against Barnsley', as Ferguson put it.

He has never forgiven us. And he is probably right.

15

End of the Dream

It used to be a game reporters played among themselves at any Leeds United press conference. How long would it be before David O'Leary mentioned 'my babies'?

There was never any money at stake, just a knowing look or a raised eyebrow between journalists as soon as O'Leary trotted out a phrase that had once been endearing but now just felt like the stalest of clichés. Any warmth that existed between manager and media was eroding as quickly as Leeds United were crumbling financially.

For a few short years, it was a compelling story of a club reborn with a manager always ready with a warm handshake and a smile, a chairman who knew the importance of a good press and a group of young stars, many of whom had grown up together in the club's academy, playing a thrilling brand of football that even had Manchester United looking over their shoulders with a sense of trepidation.

The Premier League, however, comes at you quickly. Clubs who have taken its presence for granted only need to make one bad managerial appointment, pay too much in the transfer market or ignore the laws of economics, and the Premier League bares its teeth, punishing those whose dreams outweigh reality. In truth, Leeds committed all three of those cardinal errors.

To be fair to O'Leary, he was not a bad manager, it was just that the cheery, homespun bonhomie he exuded around the media was as much of an illusion as their financial stability. I had been on the receiving end of O'Leary's ire a few years earlier when he had been left out of the Republic of Ireland squad for the World Cup in 1994 and decided to do an article with the *News of the World*, which I ghosted.

The piece, a sometimes unflattering assessment of the Ireland squad, which, according to Andy Townsend's autobiography, upset a few players, was published on the Sunday and the following Tuesday I was in the office when my phone rang. 'Paul, it's David O'Leary.'

'Hi, David, how are you?'

'Paul, you've got both my numbers in London, haven't you?'

'Yes, David.'

'Never fucking use them.' And with that the line went dead.

For several years, we didn't speak, studiously ignoring each other on the rare occasions our paths crossed socially, and while we did patch things up to the point where I interviewed him after he stepped up to replace George Graham, it always had the feeling of an uneasy truce. It was a sentiment shared by many of my colleagues who had their own experiences of the sharp side of the O'Leary tongue.

But what we could never ignore was the spectacle of the side he had built at Elland Road following Graham's departure for Spurs in September 1998. O'Leary may not have been first choice, but he was an inspired one, throwing off the shackles of Graham's defensive pragmatism and encouraging a style of football that played perfectly into the potential he had shrewdly recognised emerging from the club's academy ranks.

Howard Wilkinson's time as manager of Leeds will be

remembered most for being the last English manager to lift
the title in the season before the Premier League was born.
In West Yorkshire, he is equally regarded for instigating a
ten-year plan for a youth system at Elland Road that would
become the envy of every club, save for Manchester United.
That Wilkinson was not around at the club to witness the
culmination of his strategy does not detract from his vision
and the wisdom of appointing Paul Hart to oversee the development of so many outstanding youngsters.

If Graham was reluctant to blood many of Hart's team
that won the FA Youth Cup in 1997, O'Leary embraced them
with an almost missionary zeal. Paul Robinson, Jonathan
Woodgate and Stephen McPhail all joined Harry Kewell in
the first-team reckoning alongside Ian Harte and Lee Bowyer,
both of whom were still of an age that qualified them as one
of O'Leary's 'babies' (always 'my babies' in press conferences,
remember).

And what a team they were. They played without fear and
with a camaraderie forged from a nucleus of the team growing
up together and liking each other, not just as teammates but
as friends. Elland Road became a hot ticket for journalists,
not quite rivalling Old Trafford and the unstoppable momentum of a Treble season, but definitely worth the trip up from
London, safe in the knowledge Leeds were always a story.

There was an innocence to this side that was completely at
odds with the earliest incarnation of 'Dirty Leeds' under Don
Revie back in the seventies, and even with Wilkinson's 1992
title winners – who were more experienced, more astute and
with just the dash of flair that Eric Cantona delivered. As a
journalist, that side demanded respect, but nowhere near the
affection for the side blossoming under O'Leary.

Fourth place in O'Leary's first season in 1999 was a superb
achievement, an improvement on the previous campaign

under Graham and a return to European competition in the shape of the UEFA Cup. For chairman Peter Ridsdale it was the signal of real and fresh hope that the club he had supported as a boy, and where he had queued overnight in a sleeping bag to guarantee a ticket for the 1965 FA Cup final, was on the verge of something special.

With Ridsdale, it is always the fish tank that comes back to haunt him. Even though it cost just £240 a year to maintain, the fish tank in the chairman's office is perceived as a sign of the ruinous excess which destroyed a football club. A fish tank has come to symbolise all that was wrong with Leeds United on his watch. If it hardly seems fair, then at least it is understandable.

Because while Ridsdale was every fan's ideal chairman – a boy from the terraces who had come to run HIS club – there was always something just too good to be true about him from a reporter's standpoint, almost as if he was trying too hard to please and impress whenever you met him socially or he was being quoted in the media. And, boy, did it feel like he loved to be quoted.

Buoyed by performances both on and off the pitch where, according to the club's accounts at the time, gate receipts were up 20 per cent, television income up 40 per cent and merchandising up 13 per cent, Ridsdale saw an opportunity to take Leeds to the next level. In an interview with the *Guardian* in 2004, he said, 'There was a belief that with the right acquisitions we stood a genuine chance of challenging towards the top of the Premier League and certainly a chance of getting in the Champions League more often than not. So, what we had to do was to see how we could add to the squad in a way that would take us forward.'

It all sounds so simple.

In fact, Ridsdale and Leeds United were about to embark

on a complex labyrinth of financial transactions and schemes that, ultimately, only continued success at the highest level domestically and in Europe could facilitate. But where was the problem? The Leeds future was golden – bright young manager, bright young players, enthusiastic and supportive chairman and a small operating profit to boot – so go for it, throw everything in ... live the dream.

One area where Leeds certainly led the way was in the manipulation of far more creative financing strategies that were commonplace in business but had yet to percolate into the football world. Yet with the Premier League now established as the leading entertainment platform both at home and, increasingly, abroad as football discovered new television territories, shrewd City operatives licked their lips at the prospect of fresh markets of their own – and Leeds were at the cutting edge.

Ridsdale rejected any thought of luring wealthy benefactors to the club, not when they might have wanted a say on how their money was potentially being spent. And while their bank, HSBC, looked favourably on the club and were happy to extend spending within reasonable limits, there was nothing in the traditional banking methods that allowed for the rapid expansion Ridsdale and the board believed was needed.

So, he broke new ground in football. In short, each of the four players Leeds bought in the summer of 1999 had their transfer fee covered by a financial institution who advanced the club the exact sum, which Leeds paid back, with interest, over the term of the player's contract. The caveat was that, if the club did not keep up the payments, then the lender could force Leeds to sell the players and take proceeds of the subsequent transfer fee.

Another potential pitfall was the fact that if a player's value had fallen when he was transferred, the lender could claim the difference from the club, yet this appeared not to set any alarm bells ringing at Leeds because the whole deal was then underwritten by an insurance company, which meant, even in a worst-case scenario, the insurer would cover the lender's losses.

So simple, yet so expensive. The interest rate applied for these kinds of loans was far higher than any imposed by a traditional bank, while the exorbitant premiums to cover the insurance had to be paid in full upfront. Not that it seemed to matter to Ridsdale – and why would it, with so much confidence buzzing around the team and with the prospect of extra European nights to keep the tills ringing?

Armed with this level of financial backing, Leeds took the highest of dives into the transfer market, adding Eirik Bakke, Danny Mills, Michael Duberry and Michael Bridges to O'Leary's squad at a total cost of just over £15 million, which equated to 40 per cent of the club's total spending of £37 million for the 1998–99 season. Who, though, truly cared? English football was in the rudest of health, Manchester United had just seen off the best Europe could throw at them and Leeds were at the vanguard of those clubs whose future seemed brightest.

Even the loss of top scorer Jimmy Floyd Hasselbaink to Atletico Madrid did nothing to dampen the excitement of the new season at Elland Road, especially with Bridges quickly developing an understanding with Kewell and Alan Smith, another player who graduated with honours from the youth system and, as a Leeds fan, quickly achieved hero status.

Defeats to Manchester United and Liverpool in the first five matches were dismissed as incidental, nothing over which to lose sleep or cause concern. Elland Road was alive, a combination of fierce Yorkshire pride and giddiness at the football being served up. Ten straight home wins and an impregnable self-belief were proving an irresistible force as Leeds charged to the top of the table by the end of the year. A new millennium beckoned and, with it, surely a new era for the club.

The first fracture in the Leeds dream came twelve days into the twenty-first century amid a clatter of running feet, cries of pain and blood spilt on the Leeds city-centre streets. At the end of it, a student named Sarfraz Najeib lay unconscious, his cheekbone smashed, left leg shattered, nose broken in three places and with teeth marks and a shoe imprint scarring his face. It was a feral attack, carried out by a gang that included Woodgate and Bowyer, and the two were arrested and charged with grievous bodily harm and affray.

The arrests destroyed the carefully crafted public image of the Leeds squad. In interviews, the players – especially the youngsters – had come across as polite and humble, united in the club cause and dedicated to each other. Always punctual, always willing to give of themselves in front of a camera, microphone or notebook, the goodwill towards them from the media was immense. In the space of less than a minute, the image had been destroyed.

Now the talk was of late-night drinking, toxic masculinity, a moral vacuum fuelled by pints of vodka cocktails and visits to clubs that went by the name of DV8 and the like. For the football club, it was a public relations disaster yet, somehow, on the pitch, O'Leary maintained a sense of equilibrium.

Predictably, results dipped and four straight defeats between the end of March and the middle of April meant that any title challenge was over, but third place behind United and Arsenal meant the kind of progress Ridsdale envisaged the previous summer had come to fruition and, with it, the sunlit uplands of Champions League football the following season.

Leeds had already savoured their taste of European football with a journey to the semi-finals of the UEFA Cup, beating

Roma in the fourth round and showing a level of maturity way beyond their standing as a club and as a group that had youth at its core. Tragically, the semi-final first leg against Galatasaray was marred by the death of two Leeds fans, stabbed to death on the streets of Istanbul, which threw into doubt whether the match should even be played. These incidents inevitably affected O'Leary's team and a 2–0 first leg deficit was too much to overcome at Elland Road a fortnight later.

So, if Europe held no fears, neither did the immediate future of the club, no matter the debt that was being serviced. Their UEFA Cup campaign had brought in just shy of £7 million and qualification for the Champions League first group stage would see Leeds pocket double that. Turnover had also increased by £20 million to £57 million, which included a huge leap in both television revenue and gate receipts. On the surface, Leeds United Football Club were moving in the right direction.

And like all gamblers on a winning streak, there was no thought of consolidation from either manager or board. In all my years reporting, I have never met a manager who thinks his squad is perfectly balanced and needs no improvement, and O'Leary was no different. One defender, one midfielder and one striker were his summer demands and the board responded, sanctioning moves for Dominic Matteo, Olivier Dacourt and Mark Viduka and an outlay of £17.5 million. Business as usual.

Again, the fees were covered in the same fashion as the previous summer via sale and leaseback, with progress into the group stages giving both the Leeds board and the lenders comfort that the £15 million bounty was guaranteed from six games against Barcelona, AC Milan and Besiktas.

Those games became the major focus of attention for Leeds

fans who realised that, for all the strengthening of the previous two summers, running a Champions League campaign
and quest for domestic success was beyond the squad in terms
of both depth and experience. The adrenalin highs of trips
to the Nou Camp and San Siro could not be matched in the
bread-and-butter Premier League games and victories like the
4–3 defeat of Liverpool were few and far between.

Glittering European nights, though, were a completely different story, and what better way to prepare for the second
group stage that would include Real Madrid than pulling
off a deal that would force even the Spanish aristocrats
into a double take. A month before Christmas, Leeds broke
the transfer record for a British player that had stood since
Blackburn paid £15 million for Alan Shearer.

Ridsdale could probably justify the £18 million it took to
bring Rio Ferdinand to Yorkshire from West Ham by the fact
that doubts over Woodgate's future were uppermost in the
club's mind. With his and Bowyer's trial scheduled to start
in January 2001, there was a very real chance the defender
would be looking at a prison sentence. How the deal could be
sustained was another question entirely.

Again, some creativity was required. According to a
Guardian article by the investigative journalist Brian
Cathcart, Leeds arranged a deal whereby the monthly instal-
ments for the seven players bought on sale and leaseback
were halved, with the remaining 50 per cent being paid in a
lump sum which Cathcart describes as a 'bullet payment' at
the end of each player's contract. The Leeds board contented
themselves with the fact transfer fees were spiralling and that
with the club on a high, at least in Europe, there was little
likelihood of their players dipping in value. There was nothing
distressed about Leeds United. Well, not yet.

The start of 2001 was a startling paradox in the fortunes of a football club. Off the pitch, there were the daily unedifying reports from Hull Crown Court as Bowyer and Woodgate stood in the dock, staring at incarceration. It impacted the Leeds dressing room for more than simply the fate of the two players, as Michael Duberry first claimed Woodgate had not been on the scene and then changed his evidence to put his teammate very much at the heart of the alleged attack.

But from the court case beginning in January, a full year after the incident in question, to May 5, Leeds lost just once in the Premier League and went on an unbeaten thirteen-game run as well as marching on together in Europe. Incredibly, Bowyer was at the very heart of the success, seemingly happy to put the Crown Court behind him for ninety minutes of relief on a pitch. His form was superlative, in sharp contrast to Woodgate, whose gaunt frame and black-rimmed eyes told a story of a man beaten down by the pressure of the situation. It was exacerbated by the judge declaring a mis-trial after a prejudicial report in the *Sunday Mirror* appeared while the jury were considering their verdicts.

The trial aside, there were threatening clouds gathering on the horizon. A Champions League semi-final defeat at the hands of Valencia (less a defeat, more an education) was an amazing achievement from a team of such inexperience. But the knock-on effect of a lengthy European campaign impacted Leeds in the League and fourth spot saw them drop out of the following season's Champions League, albeit with a £20 million prize pot.

It was never going to be enough, not with the financial burden Leeds were carrying. Like somebody maxing out their credit cards to keep up with their repayments, piling debt upon debt, Leeds again went to the City for help.

A saviour appeared in the shape of Stephen Schechter, a former Wall Street banker with a track record of raising the sort of money English football had never before witnessed, let alone enjoyed. In 1999, he had helped Newcastle United secure a £50 million loan; with Leeds, he would go a step further.

On 26 September 2001, driven by Schechter's creativity, Leeds took out the biggest loan ever seen in English football: in essence, a £60 million mortgage secured against future attendances at Elland Road and the bounty of a return to the Champions League. The figures involved were astonishing; according to club accounts and detailed in the media at the time, the money was borrowed at a fixed interest rate of 7.695 per cent, with the first interest repayment coming in at £4 million. Repayment of the overall capital would not even begin until September 2004. And the cost of setting fees to arrange the loan? Just a little shy of £900,000.

Perhaps Ridsdale took confidence from the Leeds balance sheet, which showed a turnover of £86 million, gate receipts up by a third, merchandising up by 40 per cent and a doubling in television revenue received. But the operating profit of £10 million was wiped out by a wage bill that now stood at £38 million, an increase of £12 million on the previous year. The net club debt had risen by £30 million in two years and now stood at £39 million – and that was before the £60 million in new loans was literally taken into account. Leeds were standing on the precipice.

In the space of five months, they plunged into the abyss.

Leeds were not alone in using securitisation against future ticket sales; where they were different is how they spent it. Instead of long-term investment in club infrastructure, they again plunged into the transfer market, following the £11 million signing of Robbie Keane from Inter in April with moves for Robbie Fowler and Seth Johnson for a combined £21 million as well as spending £5 million on training ground improvements.

Yes, there was also a shifting of the debt structure but that was nothing more than shuffling the deckchairs on the *Titanic*.

It created the illusion of a club still able to compete both in the transfer market and on the pitch, as O'Leary led the side on an eleven-match unbeaten run, not losing in the Premier League until November. By 1 January, after a thrilling 3–0 defeat of West Ham, Leeds were top. It was never going to get any better – and it could never last.

Inevitably, the Bowyer and Woodgate court case would be the catalyst for the decline. There had been a surface tension which had held since January 2000 but that was broken in December 2001 when a jury convicted Woodgate of affray and ordered him to undertake 100 hours of community service, while Bowyer was cleared of all charges but ordered to pay almost £1 million in legal fees. What might have been a moment for quiet contemplation turned into a war of recriminations. All the emotions that had been suppressed throughout the first trial and the nine weeks of the retrial surged to the surface in a wave of destabilisation.

To his credit, Ridsdale publicly fronted a post-verdict press conference and there could be nobody who doubted his integrity. 'You can't quantify the damage that this has caused,' he said. 'None of us have wanted to go through this and, despite the fact that we, as a club, were not on trial, the mere fact that we are here today demonstrates that the two linked together and people have perceived Leeds United to be as responsible as anybody else.

'But Leeds United have not been on trial.'

Incredibly, that last sentence was utterly undermined by one simple fact: O'Leary had written a book in conjunction with the club's own director of communications. It's title? *Leeds United on Trial*.

It was the most wretchedly crass piece of opportunism since

Glenn Hoddle's World Cup diary published in the aftermath
of France 98, which destroyed any semblance of unity within
the England dressing room. To lose that level of trust at an
international level is one thing, to destroy it within a club is
unforgiveable.

The publication of the book and its serialisation in the
News of the World just forty-eight hours after the jury
returned their verdicts was met with outrage and condem-
nation in all quarters. A spokesman for the Najeib family
accused O'Leary of receiving 'blood money' in his deal with
the publishers, while James Lawton, in the *Independent*,
wrote that O'Leary had 'more faces than Eve and more positions than the Karma Sutra'.

It also smacked of the worst double standards that, while
Bowyer and Woodgate were both being fined for bringing the
club into disrepute, O'Leary was benefiting financially from
his book. It pitched the players against him, their resentment
palpable when we used to speak to agents and those closest to them.

Most importantly, it undermined the relationship between
chairman and manager. Ridsdale trod carefully in public,
admitting only that both the timing of the book and its title
had made life 'difficult', but in subsequent interviews he has
not tried to disguise his contempt for O'Leary's decision and
the manager's claims he did not know what the book was
going to be called.

As Ridsdale told *The Athletic* in 2019, 'I can only tell you,
with the benefit of hindsight, that I've since written a book
and the publishers had to agree the title with me. At the time,
I didn't believe David. And having written a book, knowing
what you go through, I now absolutely don't believe him.'

The dysfunction that had become a hallmark of the club's
financial position and internal relationships now spilled on

to the pitch and performances. From the high of New Year's Day, Leeds did not win another league game until 3 March, were bundled out of the FA Cup by Cardiff City and saw their UEFA Cup campaign ended by PSV Eindhoven. For three years, this felt like a club on an upward trajectory, but now its decline was fast becoming terminal.

With little prospect of Champions League football, even after UEFA granted England an extra place in the competition, Ridsdale and the board knew that it was time to pivot and O'Leary was told, short of a miraculous upturn in results, that players would need to be sold at the end of the season.

From press conferences I attended at the time, it was clear a rift had developed between Ridsdale and O'Leary. Publicly, O'Leary's criticism of the Leeds hierarchy was thinly veiled, while in private, once the tape recorders were turned off and the notebooks put away, he was scathing in his attacks, talking darkly of everything he had helped build being destroyed by poor financial decisions. Again, it may not have been the smartest way to win friends and influence people, but, perhaps, O'Leary was past caring.

Leeds limped through to fifth place in the Premier League, confirming the worst fears of the board as their speculate-to-accumulate strategy became nothing more than the biggest fire sale of talent seen in the Premier League era.

Inevitably, O'Leary was sacked in June, his position untenable from a results perspective and the breakdown of all the most important relationships within the club sealing his fate. Ferdinand and Keane would follow him out of Elland Road that summer, although the £37 million from their sales barely impacted the parlous financial situation where net debt was running at £82 million, the wage bill had leapt by £10 million to £53 million and debt payments totalled £1 million a month.

To witness such a desperate fall from grace was painful,

even if most of the worst wounds were self-inflicted. Senior reporters only travelled up to Elland Road from London out of some kind of macabre fascination with how quickly a mood of utter despair had set in; how a vibrant, thriving football club had fallen foul to an inexorable domino effect of destruction.

Within another transfer window, Bowyer, Woodgate, Dacourt and Fowler were sold, but, with the whole market in decline, prices fell well below what was needed as rivals, recognising a distressed foe when they saw it, simply stole away what Leeds once held dear. Ridsdale could not survive such a fall, and, in March 2003, he too left Elland Road.

What did he and O'Leary leave behind? Not the death of a football club, not quite; but certainly the death of hope, dreams, ambition and the trust between a football club and its fans.

It would take the best part of twenty years for that to be rekindled.

16

European Royalty

It is fair to say Ian Wright is excitable at the best of times. But the yell he let out in the *News of the World* hospitality box at Ascot had spectators 20 feet below us craning their necks to see what could have prompted such wild scenes.

All I can remember is Wright literally bouncing up and down, shouting, 'We've signed Dennis Bergkamp! We've signed Dennis Bergkamp!' before grabbing his phone and checking the text message that had come in from an Arsenal-supporting mate who had somehow found himself privy to this vital nugget of information.

Then there was the desperate search for the television remote control. Ceefax was clicked on to confirm that, yes, Arsenal had indeed paid £7.5 million to end Bergkamp's tortured stay in Italy. I do not recall whether Wright, a *News of the World* columnist at the time, backed any winners, but he left Ascot with a smile bigger than any punter.

Because the arrival of Bergkamp at Arsenal in the summer of 1995 still had the ability to stun the football world. Yes, the Premier League had sharpened up English football's act and invested the domestic game with a degree of glamour that had not been seen before, but that was more down to smart marketing and Sky's eye for glitzy coverage. Deep down, though, this was still a game for stout-hearted English yeoman with hearts of oak. Any discussion of foreign intervention was met with suspicion.

Scandinavians were okay because, well, they all spoke good English, played a very similar style of robust football and had a reputation as strong characters who could fit into a dressing room with ease in the way that Peter Schmeichel did at Manchester United or Henning Berg at Blackburn Rovers. As Ray Harford, assistant to Kenny Dalglish at Ewood Park, once told me, 'Swedes and Danes are perfect. They settle like snow, speak the language, train perfectly and look after their bodies – I'd have them all day long.'

The only person to have bucked the trend was Eric Cantona, whose presence at both Leeds and Manchester United was seen as a one-off, a maverick to whom French football had turned its back and so England was almost a last resort for his talents. No matter that he revolutionised the mentality at Old Trafford with his exacting standards and dedication to training, Cantona was an outlier and not the trailblazer for a new foreign orthodoxy.

Even the biggest names had to fight to be accepted in the English game. Jürgen Klinsmann already had a World Cup winner's medal to his name from Italia 90, had just scored five goals for newly unified Germany in the 1994 World Cup and was considered one of the finest strikers on the planet. But did we want him in the Premier League? What, a German? And a cheating German to boot, with his theatrical diving antics? No thanks.

The backlash against Tottenham's decision to bring Klinsmann from Monaco (where he did not agree with the coaching methods of a certain Arsène Wenger) was immense. The parochial Little Englander mentality so very easily tipped towards outright xenophobia among the media, fans and even those in the game whose cynicism knew no bounds. '£1m A YEAR FOR A DIVE BOMBER' screamed the headline in the *Daily Mirror*, while too many other news outlets relied on tired Second World War tropes to suggest why Klinsmann would never be welcome in the Premier League.

Not that Klinsmann seemed overly perturbed; smart, savvy and possessing a sense of humour that immediately subverted all the righteous indignation that greeted his arrival, he opened his unveiling press conference with a question to the assembled media. 'Does anybody know if there is a diving school in London?' he enquired, with a look of pure innocence, following it up with the news that he was planning to tour the capital in his VW Beetle, taking in all the sights, just like any other enraptured tourist.

It was a move of public relations genius and when he celebrated his first Tottenham goal with a full swallow dive accompanied by several teammates, even those who condemned this foreign interloper were won over. His twenty-nine goals that season earned him the Footballer of the Year crown voted by the Football Writers' Association, yet still there was the belief this was just a fleeting moment, an episode clouded in novelty value, underlined by the fact Klinsmann and his Beetle lasted just a year at White Hart Lane before returning home to Bayern Munich.

That is why Arsenal's capture of Bergkamp felt so significant. While Klinsmann had been thirty when he arrived at Spurs and very definitely in the winding-down stage of his career, Bergkamp was four years younger and memories were still fresh of the fabulously deft volley against England at Wembley two years earlier, a goal that Wright gushed over in the box at Ascot on the day the news broke of Arsenal's coup.

Yet still we (and I use the word advisedly because I was not short of an opinion or two in print) only wanted to search for the negatives. Instead of celebrating a player whose poise, vision and speed of thought and movement should have been a welcome antidote to the collision-course football that was still the staple of Premier League football, we chose to nit-pick. Two years of failure in Italy's Serie A were enough to convince us that Bergkamp had nothing to offer the English game, that his effete stylishness had no place over here – and six games without a goal strengthened the prosecution's case.

Looking back now, it seems ridiculous we could ever have doubted Bergkamp's pedigree or even suggested English football was no place for such a talent. Some of that stems from an insularity, some from an arrogance that the world had nothing to offer us now that the Premier League was the richest league in the world and where hyperbole was the currency in which we in the media dealt. We were long overdue an education and, thankfully, there were two Dutchmen perfectly positioned to hand out a lesson.

Two goals against Southampton in his seventh game heralded a turn in Bergkamp's fortunes and from then on, he was imperious. While across the capital, a fellow countryman was displaying all the swagger Chelsea fans demanded.

Like Klinsmann the year before, Ruud Gullit's career was in decline, and he was some way removed from his days at AC Milan, where he was arguably the finest player on the planet as the Italian side dominated Europe, with Gullit alongside compatriots Marco van Basten and Frank Rijkaard. Glenn Hoddle's vision for Gullit was as a true sweeper, unencumbered by marking duties at the back, free to step in and launch attacks from deep, a presence unrivalled even at the age of thirty-two.

Sam Rush is the chief executive of the General Sports Europe agency and a former CEO of Derby County. In the early nineties, he played a key role at SFX, the agency that represented the likes of David Beckham, Alan Shearer, Michael Owen and David Platt. He looked on with fascination at the developing trends ushered in by the advent of the Premier League, especially the influx of foreign talent that may have started as a trickle but was soon to become an unstoppable torrent.

'In the early days, there were two main reasons why a player wanted to come to England,' Rush recalls. 'Well, three, because you cannot take money out of the equation completely. But for the likes of Klinsmann and Gullit, wages were never the overriding factor because, frankly, they had already made their fortunes in the game.

'For those two players, it was a case of a new frontier at a time in their careers when they wanted to enjoy life and have an element of fun. The reach of the Premier League was such that it was an enticing prospect to European players, it wasn't simply packaged for the domestic market, it was being seen in Italy, in Spain, in Germany, in France and it was something fresh and exciting, a different challenge.

'Then with, say, Bergkamp, it was a chance to prove himself all over again. Everybody knew that he was a sensational player but those two years at Inter Milan, where he had struggled for goals and the paucity of chances that came his way, had dented his reputation and probably his confidence and I think he desperately needed a new stage and a chance to fall back in love with the game.

'Plus, the English game was exciting and attacking. It may not have been the best technical league, but it was played in front of full grounds that, following the Taylor Report, were becoming some of the best in the world with the all-seater redevelopments. You should never underestimate the attraction of packed grounds for players because, outside of the top teams in Italy and Spain – where the old money was – sometimes you'd be playing in front of just a few thousand supporters with an atmosphere to match.

'London was also a magnet because it is a magnificent place to live but it was never the be-all and end-all of the attraction. Thanks to the astonishing television deals, there were clubs up and down the country who were looking abroad to a new market for players – and players weren't scared to live somewhere other than London, they just wanted to be in a country that felt like it was on the verge of something extraordinary.'

Extraordinary seems an apt description for a move four months after Bergkamp's arrival that bucked the general trend. This was not a player approaching the twilight of his career, looking for one last adventure, nor was it somebody with a reputation to repair, needing a fresh challenge. This was a bone fide superstar – and he had his heart set on Middlesbrough.

In the summer of 1995, England under Terry Venables took part in the Umbro Cup tournament that also included Brazil, Sweden and Japan. It was a warm-up for the following year's European Championships which were to be held on home soil and saw England play three games in the space of a week, culminating in a clash with Brazil at Wembley.

As Pele took his place in the Royal Box, all eyes were on the slight figure who had inherited the great man's number 10 shirt. A teenage Ronaldo may have started up front for Brazil, but it was Juninho who ran the show with his intelligence, movement and ability to mesmerise with a ball at his feet. His was the quintessential Brazilian performance, a 25-yard free kick which flicked up and over the England wall and inside the left-hand post for an equaliser before sliding in Ronaldo with a pass of exquisite weight and pace for Brazil's second in a 3–1 victory.

The world sat up and took notice, but one man who paid

special attention was sat on the England bench. Bryan Robson was assistant to Venables and also manager of Middlesbrough, newly promoted to the Premier League after winning the Championship and determined to make an impact on the top flight in their new Riverside Stadium home, a massive upgrade on decrepit Ayresome Park.

It helped that chairman Steve Gibson was, in the days before oligarchs and petrol billionaires, one of the richest owners in the Premier League, with a devotion to his child-hood club that bordered on the fanatical. He was a manager's dream: a chairman who gave unstinting backing in the transfer market and who wanted to dispel the lazy imagery of Boro as nothing more than a northern backwater, lacking in anything approaching glamour.

Adrian Bevington would go on to become managing director of Club England at the FA, helping to select England managers across all age groups, but back in 1995 he was a senior member of Middlesbrough's communications team. He watched with increasing incredulity as the club pulled off one of the transfer coups of the decade.

'Bryan had his eye on Juninho from the Wembley game. The club was determined to land him and beat off the competition from bigger clubs, so Bryan and the chief executive, Keith Lamb, flew down to Sao Paulo to meet Juninho and his family first, not leaving until they got him.

'The fact they were on the ground and willing to make the trip themselves meant a lot to Juninho and his family. You also have to remember Bryan was a huge name in world football and an incredibly impressive figure, which really helped.'

With an open line to Gibson back in England, it meant the Boro party could make quick decisions and negotiate properly without too many complications. Without the world knowing too much of what was happening, Juninho agreed personal details, underwent a medical in a local hospital and had even picked out a house before boarding a flight to London. It was a surreal moment, watching Brazil's number 10, wrapped in a coat bigger than him, arriving in Middlesbrough with a grinning Gibson waiting to welcome him.

Not quite as surreal as Juninho's first press conference when one of the first questions was about how he would cope with the north-east winters and their biting North Sea winds and blizzards. Always considerate and polite, Juninho gave a lengthy answer in Portuguese which his interpreter analysed before simply responding, 'It will not be a problem.'

And it was never a problem. He may have taken a little while to acclimatise to the English game but with his parents and sister in England for support, Juninho was a stunning success. His slight frame belied a strength on the ball and an ability to withstand even the most rugged of challenges and, like Gullit at Chelsea, it felt like the Brazilian was a thought process ahead of both teammates and opponents. His arrival opened the Premier League beyond even the boundaries of Europe in a way that had not been seen since 1978 when Ossie Ardiles and Ricky Villa barely had time to celebrate Argentina's World Cup victory before signing for Spurs.

Even with everything in its favour in terms of spectacle, finance and the ability to attract some of the game's stellar names, the Premier League still had one more card to add to its already impressive hand, courtesy of what started as an obscure legal challenge but culminated in a decision that would irrevocably change the business model of football.

In 1990, Jean-Marc Bosman began a court case claiming his rights under the 1957 Treaty of Rome, which allowed for freedom of movement in Europe, had been violated. He claimed that, at the end of his contract with RFC Liege, he was prevented from moving clubs after the Belgian side demanded a prohibitive transfer fee. The case predated the Premier League by two years but when, in 1995, Bosman finally won in the European Court of Justice, it was a decision that would have an astonishing impact on the Premier League and beyond.

In its very basic terms, 'doing a Bosman' allowed a player to run down his contract and leave on a free transfer at the end of the current deal. Any club that wanted to sign that player no longer had to find a transfer fee and, in theory, could offer a vastly favourable salary package from the money saved.

Jon Smith and his brother Phil had formed the First Artist agency in 1986 and had represented Diego Maradona and the England football team among a glittering roster of talent. First Artist had done the deal to bring Gullit to Chelsea and were key players in the world of high-profile transfers.

For Smith, the Bosman ruling created opportunities for players and agents alike to grow exponentially, as he explains: 'We knew Bosman had a serious case and he had a very tenacious lawyer called Jean-Louis Dupont who I had the privilege of meeting on a few occasions.

'Suddenly, you had the option of running your player's contract down to zero with no transfer fee and another club could have them for nothing. If you had a decent agent, they'd say, "Hang on, you're not paying any millions for him, we want a little bit more on the signing fee, we want a little bit more on the wages or WE want a little bit more."

'Then the clubs had to balance out if they had a player on that much wage, how [that compared] with everyone else. So very often it went on signing-on bonuses, it was constant juggling of figures and juxtaposing of contracts. A really exciting time because everything was new and different.'

While the players may have enjoyed a reframing of the power balance, it still allowed Premier League clubs, with their strong bottom line bolstered by a game-changing television deal, to dangle some of the most lucrative contracts under the noses of players who, now, were not costing eye-watering amounts. Whereas the likes of Paul Gascoigne, David Platt and Des Walker had all been lured away from the English game to Italy, now English clubs could happily shop in Rome, Milan and Genoa with the kind of spending power they had never had before.

Six months after the Bosman ruling came into effect, I was in Rome for the Champions League final between Juventus and Ajax, and out of the twenty-eight players who actually set foot on the pitch, twelve would, at some time or other, play for Premier League clubs. But, in truth, there was only one story that night – the departure for England of two of the biggest names in Italian football.

Gianluca Vialli and Fabrizio Ravanelli played their last games for Juventus, Vialli hoisting the trophy as captain and Ravanelli scoring for Turin's Old Lady. Both were coy after the game, not wanting to puncture the euphoria of victory, but Vialli, in particular, was under fire from the Italian media to reveal WHY he was daring to leave Juve and, secondly, WHERE he was going.

Frankly, both were the worst-kept secrets in football. Vialli was leaving on a Bosman free for Chelsea and the reason was simple: the lure of London and a hugely lucrative final move in a career that had seen him scale the heights of Italian football. What else was there for him in Serie A now that Juventus had claimed the Champions League crown? Why not sample life in London?

Ravanelli was a different creature altogether. A cultural experience appeared to be the last thing on his mind, all he wanted was a taste of the riches the Premier League could offer. After the final in Rome, he fought through a crowd of reporters all desperate for a nugget of information as to his next club but all they got in response was, 'I don't know, I don't know.'

Middlesbrough were one of the clubs in contention for his signature yet, as Adrian Bevington admits, there was no over-whelming appetite for Teesside on Ravanelli's part. 'I'm not sure Ravanelli really wanted to leave Juventus that summer, but he walked into a Turin meeting room to find Bryan and Keith Lamb, who had – as I understand – already agreed terms on a £7 million deal.

'The deal was a closely guarded secret within the club and came as a brilliant shock to most of us when we were told the news. It was a massive power play and the excitement levels when Rav signed went through the roof.'

The love affair with Ravanelli was hardly mutual. While Vialli embraced London life, revelled in the freedom his move had brought him and assimilated seamlessly into the Premier League, Ravanelli barely tolerated his new surroundings, carped incessantly about the poor training facilities, the weather (both with good reason) and the town itself (with no justification whatsoever). In short, a hat-trick against Liverpool on the opening day of the season was about the only true highlight of Ravanelli's brief one-season stay at the Riverside. That, and the fact that his £42,000-a-week wages made him the highest paid player in Premier League history to that point.

If Ravanelli had embodied Alan Sugar's sneering denun-ciation of foreign players as 'Carlos Kickaball' mercenaries, he was the exception rather than the rule. Juninho had been joined at Middlesbrough by two other Brazilians, Emerson and Branco, who, unlike Ravanelli, assimilated into north-east life without a murmur of complaint, as had David Ginola and Philippe Albert in Newcastle, while, heading south,

Tony Yeboah and Benito Carbone were perfectly at home in Yorkshire with Leeds and Sheffield Wednesday respectively, as was Igor Štimac at Derby.

Predictably, though, it was London that was home to the bulk of that first wave of foreign imports. Fresh from a spectacularly successful Euro 96 tournament played out in brilliant sunshine for the most part, Britpop London was taking on a cultural significance unrivalled across the continent, while Tony Blair's New Labour energy was creating a mood of optimism and hope that had become intertwined with the spectacle of the Premier League. Footballers were rock stars, while all rock stars wanted to do was kick a ball and rub shoulders with the players.

Vialli was joined at Chelsea by compatriots Roberto Di Matteo and Gianfranco Zola, as well as Frenchman Frank Leboeuf. In North London, Arsène Wenger's arrival at Highbury had been presaged by the signings of Patrick Vieira and Remi Garde, one who would go on to become one of the finest players of his generation and the other who played a vital role in helping the young Vieira to settle and learn the language.

Within two years, the Premier League had gone from, in the words of Wenger, 'monoculture to multi-cultural' in barely the time it takes to make a decent cappuccino.

With it came an inevitable rise in standards – not just in matches, but in terms of preparation. Just as Cantona had effected change at Old Trafford with his attention to detail, devotion to training-ground perfection and embrace of nutrition, so the new imports changed the mindset of their clubs.

Chelsea's old training ground at Harlington was so close to Heathrow's runways that sessions had to stop every time Concorde took off because no manager could be heard over the noise of a supersonic jet. It was a wind-blown, desolate place, even in the height of summer, with changing rooms and facilities barely worthy of a non-league team. Historically, Chelsea players spent as little time there as possible, often not even bothering to shower at the end of a session.

Yet from the moment Gullit replaced Glenn Hoddle as manager and brought in so many continental stars – in particular Zola – Harlington buzzed. Di Matteo and Zola would stay out practising free kicks and would be joined by Dennis Wise. Leboeuf could be seen going through a strenuous stretching routine at the end of a session while Vialli would, more often than not, be on the massage table.

Success was immediate, with Chelsea winning the FA Cup in Gullit's first season and following it up with the European Cup Winners' Cup the following year, while Arsenal under Wenger were building to something quite spectacular.

And still they came. Emmanuel Petit, Nicolas Anelka and Marc Overmars at Arsenal, Paolo Di Canio at Sheffield Wednesday, Marcel Desailly and Didier Deschamps at Chelsea, Jimmy Floyd Hasselbaink at Leeds; the list was as impressive as the influx was relentless. Yes, there was the occasional dud and mercenary but that was inevitable with the sheer weight of numbers arriving on these shores.

There was also the occasional outcry that English football was losing its soul, and subsequent England managers, from Hoddle through to Kevin Keegan and Sven-Göran Eriksson, would labour the point that they had fewer and fewer players to choose from. But who at the top of the Premier League or even among the twenty chairmen was going to try to hold back the tide when overseas broadcasting rights had leapt from £40 million in 1992 to £98 million five years later, driven in large part by the presence of international superstars?

Fittingly, it was Chelsea who created Premier League history when Vialli, who had replaced Gullit as manager at

Stamford Bridge, named the first team to start without an Englishman in its ranks when they faced Southampton on Boxing Day 1999.

Holland, Spain, France, Brazil, Nigeria, Romania, Italy, Uruguay and Norway were all represented in what was the perfect embodiment of the dream on which the Premier League had been built; the pre-eminent football competition driven by a global passion and a hunger for English football, funded by record-breaking commercial deals and delivering a spectacle of true quality.

(And if you could name Ed de Goey, Albert Ferrer, Frank Leboeuf, Emerson Thome, Celestine Babayaro, Dan Petrescu, Gabriele Ambrosetti, Roberto Di Matteo, Gus Poyet, Didier Deschamps and Tore André Flo as that all-foreign Chelsea XI, take a house point.)

17

Riches from the East

Amid the controversy and recriminations of his ownership, it is difficult to remember that the overriding reaction to Roman Abramovich's arrival in English football was one of sheer bloody excitement.

I was at Stamford Bridge on that day in the summer of 2003 when Abramovich walked through the doors as official owner for the first time and, away from actual football matches, it felt like the most game-changing moment I had covered as a reporter since the actual formation of the Premier League eleven years earlier.

It felt historic. It felt defining. I joined two fellow journalists and dozens of Chelsea fans at the entrance to the Bridge reception, hoping to grab a glimpse of the Russian billionaire who had arrived unheralded into the heart of our game and, perhaps, a word for our readers.

I was working on the *Sunday People* at the time and needed something different from the daily story of his actual takeover, I needed to put some flesh on the bones or glean even the merest insight into the character of the man who had replaced Ken Bates as the overlord in London SW6. Rob Beasley from the *News of the World* and Paul Smith of the *Sunday Mirror* were alongside me and as we saw Abramovich leave his limousine and head for the door, we stuck our elbows out in true tabloid fashion and attempted to ambush him.

Fat chance. We probably got within 10 feet of him before a phalanx of bodyguards calmly but effectively herded us away. I think it was Rob who shouted in his general direction, 'Roman, are you happy to be at Chelsea?' and received a thumbs-up and a smile for his efforts. And that was as close as anybody in the English football media got to an interview in nineteen years.

We should have known we were on a hiding to nothing. Earlier that day, the media had packed into one of the hospitality lounges at the ground, waiting to meet and greet members of Abramovich's entourage – at least, the ones who were permitted to speak on his behalf, not the members of his inner sanctum who would never deign to offer a syllable either on or off the record.

John Mann, Abramovich's hugely likeable spokesman, had flown in from Moscow for the occasion and a few of us manoeuvred him into a quiet corner, away from the main throng of reporters, and asked him what the chances were of Abramovich giving the papers an interview, you know, once he had got his feet under the table at Chelsea.

'Not a chance,' Mann smiled.

'What, not even if Chelsea win the Champions League?' someone joked.

'Not even if they win their fifth Champions League,' Mann responded. 'You will never sit down with him, that just won't happen.'

Never knowingly taking no for an answer, reporters continued to push their luck. Chelsea's first Premier League game of the Abramovich era was at Liverpool on 17 August and the new man had flown in from his home in the South of France to be on Merseyside. To get from the Anfield directors' box to the lounge, you have to pass by the side of the press box, and it was there that one of my colleagues planned to make his move.

John Edwards, then of the *Daily Mail*, is not the tallest of men but he virtually flung himself up and on to the side of the press box to precariously hang there, arm outstretched clasping a tape recorder, asking Abramovich his views on a 2–1 victory and what his plans for Chelsea were. Abramovich at first looked confused, then looked towards his security guards, a clue for John to beat a hasty retreat.

Mind you, the media did not exactly need an interview with the main man when his actions were filling the papers, television news and radio broadcasts every single day. It was what rolling news was built for, the constant update on Chelsea stories and Abramovich's rouble-fuelled trolley dash through the European leagues for their prized assets.

It was all in such stark contrast to his entrance into the Premier League. Everybody in the game knew that Chelsea were in a dire financial position after Ken Bates had taken out a Eurobond for £75 million to fund the purchase of the freehold of Stamford Bridge, as well as building hotels, restaurants and a health club on the site. It was an ambitious plan, carried out with all the usual Bates bristling bravado but one that cut Chelsea perilously close to the bone and only qualification for the Champions League on the last day of the 2002–03 season helped stave off immediate disaster.

Bates makes for a fearful foe but a wonderful friend and, having made the journey from enemy to somebody who I liked to think of as more than just a contact, it was painful to see him and the club in such a stricken position. Chelsea chief executive Trevor Birch had been tasked with outlining new funding options and/or investors and, being an insolvency expert by trade, had come up with several strategies to ease the club's burden.

One route was via football's new friend Stephen Schechter, who had introduced both Newcastle and Leeds United to securitisation deals: basically, mortgaging season ticket sales for the next twenty-five years in return for an upfront sum of around £120 million. No doubt Bates had seen the ramifications for Leeds and their headlong spiral towards financial ruin and opted against that particular path.

He also refused to give up control of the club, which appeared to rule out a sale to a financial institution who would, no doubt, have wanted their own man running Chelsea on a day-to-day basis, something Bates would always have struggled to countenance.

The last option was more attractive but shaded towards the short term. Paul Taylor, a property tycoon, suggested a £10 million investment by taking advantage of a new thirty million share issue and making a loan to the club based on revenue received from Chelsea's slice of the Sky broadcast deal. That would have given Bates breathing space until August, after which another round of funding would have been required.

Little did Bates realise at the time that his saviour had already flown overhead.

As with much of the Abramovich backstory, it is sometimes difficult to separate legend from fact. His advocates – and while they are few and far between these days, there were plenty in 2003 – will tell you he had attended the World Cup both in France in 1998 and in Japan and Korea four years later. What is certain is that Abramovich was lifted from his seat in terms of excitement just a few months before he bought Chelsea when he watched Manchester United take on Real Madrid in the Champions League at Old Trafford.

Having been fortunate enough to be a spectator at the same game, it was impossible not to be enraptured by some of the greatest players on the planet, a Ronaldo hat-trick (Brazilian not Cristiano) and a superlative David Beckham free kick in a 4–3 victory for United that still was not enough to see them past Madrid's Galacticos over two legs. You would have needed a heart of Russian granite not to be moved.

Folklore has it that that game whetted the Abramovich appetite for football ownership and, in the company of super-agent Pini Zahavi, he discussed how he might go about buying a club and, just as importantly, where. Spain and Italy were complicated by the fact that even the biggest clubs have an element of either fan ownership or boardroom presence; there was nothing overly glamorous about Germany or France at the time, and South America was too far away to be practical. Which left England.

According to Keith Harris, the former chairman of the Football League and an investment banker who specialised in football takeovers, United were dismissed as being difficult to improve either on the football side or commercially, Arsenal's demand for a new ground at the time was prohibitively expensive, while Tottenham needed the kind of squad investment that was impossible to achieve in the space of the two transfer windows Abramovich had immediately targeted.

But one day, as Abramovich's helicopter was following the course of the Thames, he apparently spotted a football stadium and asked an adviser who played there. The answer? Chelsea.

'There was a great deal of research done by him and his advisers before going to Chelsea,' Harris, who was involved in the deal, told *The Times* in July 2003. 'He looked at a number of other clubs – Manchester United, Arsenal and Tottenham Hotspur – but I can understand why he chose Chelsea. The assets are in place, and they have spent a lot of money developing the ground into one of the best in the Premier League. The infrastructure of the team is good and although money needs to be spent on it, the backbone is strong.'

He could have added that Bates was desperate, which made any potential deal all the more straightforward – and speedy.

Zahavi was already aware from discussions with Birch that Chelsea was an option for Abramovich's billions and that a straight cash deal could be facilitated as swiftly as was necessary should Abramovich want to proceed. In late June, Birch again met Zahavi and the first chapter of the deal was written before, three days later, Abramovich himself met Birch at the Bridge.

Birch was astonished at the directness of Abramovich's move. Within the space of an hour, a share price of 35p had been agreed, valuing the club at £60 million, with Abramovich happy to take on the £80 million club debt. Not exactly the kind of money you find down the side of a settee, even as a billionaire, but for a football club occupying the most expensive real estate in the Premier League and who already had a team good enough to qualify for a place among Europe's elite, it feels like a bargain.

Bargain or not, Bates shook hands on the deal later than night and the next morning it was announced to the world that Chelsea had become only the second Premier League club to fall into the hands of a foreign owner, following Mohamed Al-Fayed's acquisition of Fulham six years earlier.

On the morning of 2 July, Matthew Garrahan of the *Financial Times* sat in one of the Millennium Suites which hold pride of place at Stamford Bridge, awaiting the rarest of journalistic opportunities: an audience with Abramovich. I have been jealous of many people before but, looking back, never have I been more envious of a fellow reporter than I was of Matthew.

Even now, when I am asked who I would have loved to have interviewed but never had the opportunity, I will always say Abramovich. To be able to speak with the person who, alongside Rupert Murdoch, changed the global fabric of a sport and the way we view it would be unmissable. I am very much aware of the dark side of Abramovich's story, the allegations of overseeing a corrupt process that exploited Russia's mineral wealth and the path that led to his billions, but that can never dilute my journalistic fascination with the man himself. I am pretty sure the overwhelming percentage of my colleagues would say the same.

Instead, we can only sit back and accept that Garrahan belongs in an elite group from our profession given any kind of time with Abramovich. So why Chelsea? It would be satisfying to think there was some degree of romance involved; instead, it was far more simplistic, as Abramovich explained to the *FT*: 'We did a detailed analysis over a number of months on the clubs we were interested in, and Chelsea had the most pluses and was the most ideal. I thought I could bring a lot of pluses, too.

'I don't look at this as a financial investment, I look at it as a hobby, as a sport rather than an investment. I'm looking at it as something to have fun with rather than having to realise a return. In Russia, England is always viewed as a very good place, with its education culture being of high calibre.

'It's pleasant to be here, you feel comfortable, and you don't feel people are watching you. I'm sure people will focus on me for three or four days, but it will pass. They'll forget who I am, and I like that.'

How wrong can one man be? Nineteen years later and he is still the focus of attention.

In fact, the first four days were probably the quietest of the whole Abramovich era. It was after then that the waves he would continue making for the best part of two decades throughout English football were first witnessed.

Within a week, the England manager, Sven-Göran Eriksson, was forced to deny he was about to turn his back on the Football Association and replace Claudio Ranieri as boss at the Bridge after news leaked that he had met with Abramovich and Zahavi in London. Eriksson's explanation that this was just a 'social meeting' was greeted with a sense of outright cynicism by many at the FA and, as one member of their media team told a few of us at the time, 'Sven has this unfortunate habit of bumping into club owners just when they're looking to replace their managers.' Given that a year before he had been tipped to take over from Sir Alex Ferguson at United before the Scot decided to stay on, it was easy to see why there was such suspicion within FA corridors.

But if Abramovich could not lure the manager he wanted, he had no such problems attracting players to Chelsea. Eleven arrived that first summer, with Glen Johnson being first through the door on 15 July. West Ham's pain at losing a star defender was eased a little when the full £6 million transfer fee was deposited in the club account in one go, rather than the usual payments over the course of the contract. Abramovich was making both players AND rivals very rich, very quickly.

After Johnson came Geremi from Real Madrid, Wayne Bridge, Damien Duff and Joe Cole. Then muscles were truly flexed in London as Juan Sebastián Verón was snatched away from Old Trafford before Europe was raided for Adrian Mutu, Alexey Smertin, Hernán Crespo and Claude Makélélé.

Literally in the space of a month, Abramovich had spent £110 million, with poor old Neil Sullivan, the goalkeeper beaten by Beckham from the halfway line seven years previously, the only man who did not cost a seven-figure sum. Instead, he became the rarest of beasts at Chelsea – a free transfer.

The summer transfer window, especially for Sunday news-papers, is a joy for the football journalism industry. Every whisper, rumour and conversation with an agent or manager is lapped up by fans desperate for any clue as to their club's next target or signing. Frankly, at the *People*, we could have filled every page with speculation as to who Chelsea would be signing next to the point where we had a policy: unless we were absolutely convinced they would be putting pen to paper in the next forty-eight hours, everything else was just white noise and added nothing to the paper's credibility.

But amid the multi-million-pound signings and the bonanza days for the fans as they contemplated their own club version of fantasy football, there was a ruthlessness about Abramovich and the new Chelsea regime that became appar-ent as the briefing against Ranieri became an almost daily occurrence, even before a ball had been kicked. No manager in Premier League history had been such a hot favourite for the sack before his team had even set foot on the pitch.

While Ranieri's future was a source of speculation, there was no such doubt over Trevor Birch. The man who had done so much to save Chelsea was shown the door and Peter Kenyon was ushered in, the former Manchester United chief executive promising he would help Chelsea 'turn the world blue' commercially. If that was met with justifiable cynicism in many quarters, there was also the suspicion that Abramovich might just be the man to help Kenyon realise his lofty ambition.

Not that the new Chelsea owner had everything his own way in those early days. Part of the Ken Bates masterplan had been to build the Millennium Suites in the Bridge's West

Stand: a cluster of hospitality boxes that were the envy of the rest of the Premier League for their luxury appointment and the service on offer. I have been fortunate to be invited into one or other of the boxes a handful of times over the past twenty years and the experience is beyond privileged.

Abramovich was certainly impressed and earmarked the box that looked exactly over the halfway line: the best view in the house. The only problem was that Sky had paid £10 million for a ten-year lease and, ever so politely, refused to give it up, no matter who was asking. So Abramovich had to settle for the box next door, and it always felt just a little perverse that when Sky invited me to a game a couple of times in the suite, the billionaire owner was forced to sit just to the right of the perfect position. As soon as Sky's lease expired, Abramovich swooped and the two adjoining suites formed his inner sanctum on match days.

Abramovich was also about to discover that, no matter the number of zeroes on your bank balance, it does not guarantee you success in the Premier League, especially when you are up against a rival striving to create history.

There is a chapter in this book dedicated entirely to Arsène Wenger's Invincibles and their achievement. Against a team that were about to go unbeaten in the league, any manager would have struggled to forge a Chelsea side into a cohesive unit from the tsunami of new faces that arrived in the summer – plus Scott Parker, who was signed for £13 million from Charlton when the transfer window reopened in January.

But when Kenyon arrived in February 2004, after serving six months gardening duty, he did little to alleviate the pressure on Ranieri. In his first interview, he laid down the marker. 'If you leave the investment aside, it will be a huge disappointment if we don't win anything and I'm sure the fans would agree with that,' Kenyon said. 'If you include the investment, however, it will be a failure if we don't win anything.

'That's the way the manager will see it and the way we see it because we expect to win things – that's what we do.'

Ranieri was on notice – much to the disgust of Bates, who felt similarly slighted over the way his Chelsea legacy was now being whitewashed out of history by a culture that appeared to have no time for the past. Personal experience told me that if you push Bates too far, you should expect a savaging: only a £600 lunch in Copenhagen and a personal apology had saved me from a lawsuit after I had made some disparaging – and false – remarks about the old man. He was not about to be so forgiving with Abramovich.

In true Bates fashion, he saved his ire for a very public occasion in front of a two-hundred-strong audience at one of his Supper Club events. He pulled no punches: 'When I signed the contract with Roman Abramovich, certain things were agreed. It was anticipated that there would be a phased phase-out, but it has not gone the way I anticipated it would do.

'Without apportioning blame to either party, I have decided it's a clash between Eastern and Western cultures. Their values are not my values. Their standards are not my standards. It's in the best interest of the club. It's better that Peter Kenyon operates the club in his own way without me being on the sidelines.'

In truth, Kenyon had Abramovich's blessing to run Chelsea the way he saw fit, with or without the presence of Bates, but for many Chelsea fans, the departure of the man who, himself, had saved the club from property developers during his twenty-two-year tenure and had brought a relative level of success to SW6 raised questions over the direction in which Chelsea were heading.

The reignited chase for Eriksson did little to dissuade those same fans that Chelsea, the richest club in the world, felt the normal rules of engagement did not apply to them.

As Chelsea fell way off the title pace, left in Arsenal's invincible slipstream, Eriksson was invited to Kenyon's London apartment in late March, where the pair were captured by a photographer from the *Sun*, an image shot through a curtain but strong enough to be blazoned across the front page.

It started another feeding frenzy which centred not only on Eriksson's audacity but also on the sheer nerve of Chelsea doing their best to unsettle a man who was due to lead the country in a World Cup a little over a year down the line. If it was an attempt to force Eriksson to commit to Chelsea, it was a cack-handed one and ultimately unsuccessful: forty-eight hours later, the Swede signed a new contract with the FA and Abramovich was left with his own manager who knew without a doubt nothing could save him given the very public search for a successor.

Could Ranieri have survived if he had won the Champions League, where Chelsea had made it through to a quarter-final against Arsenal? I doubt it. Subsequent history tells us Abramovich fired even the most successful managers if they fell below the standards expected, so I cannot see any way Ranieri would have been different – even if he had brought silverware to the Bridge at the first time of asking under the new regime.

In the event, Ranieri made it easy for Abramovich with one of the most bizarre series of managerial decisions witnessed in Chelsea's history. Having beaten Arsenal in the quarter-finals, Chelsea were pitched against Monaco and installed as favourites to make it through to the final.

Ranieri, though, decided that if this game was going to be his valediction, he would at least leave Chelsea with a vision of what a tactical genius they were losing. The decisions he made through a tortuous ninety minutes for Abramovich were compounded by the one in the build-up to the game when he spoke to the Spanish sports paper, *Marca*, criticising his owner for underestimating the job Ranieri had done with such an expensive but hastily delivered squad of players. Sadly, for the manager, that myth was exploded on the Côte d'Azur.

Level at 1–1 with a man advantage after Monaco's Andreas Zikos was sent off, all Chelsea had to do was remain sensible and composed and the least they could expect was a valuable away goal to take back to London. Instead, and against all his conservative principles, Ranieri gambled, throwing on a striker, Jimmy Floyd Hasselbaink, for a right back in Mario Melchiot. Then, when it became clear Chelsea were unbalanced, Ranieri put on Robert Huth, a centre half, at right back and sacrificed Parker from midfield. It was as shambolic as it was perplexing, and Monaco exploited the chaos with two goals in the last thirteen minutes.

The return leg at the Bridge was basically Ranieri's last hurrah. Chelsea scampered into a 2–0 lead which would have been enough to secure a place in the final thanks to that away goal in Monaco but there was never any confidence they could hold out, so shattered did Chelsea appear once Monaco turned on the pressure. The French side scored and scored again for a 5–3 aggregate victory and a place in the final.

Sitting in the Stamford Bridge stands that night was the man to whom Abramovich would turn less than a month later after he fired Ranieri, a figure who would give the owner the success and status he ultimately craved but whose presence would lead to the kind of fallout from which only one man would survive.

And that man was not going to be José Mourinho.

18

Close To Perfect

Gordon Strachan is on his feet. 'Wherever you are on the planet, you will not be watching football played any better than this,' he proclaims.

Where we are on the planet is the press box at Highbury with Strachan in his role as a pundit for BBC 5 Live's coverage of Arsenal versus Aston Villa. Anybody who has ever dealt with him as a player, manager or even just socially will happily confirm the fact there is nobody less given to hyperbole. He can be sandpaper dry in his wit and caustic comments, but not once would you ascribe him as gushing in his praise for anything.

Yet here he is, standing in appreciation of what is being unveiled in front of those of us privileged to be in attendance. It is mesmeric. It is astonishing. Frighteningly, it is what we have come to expect from this Arsenal side.

For the previous forty-nine Premier League games, they have swept all in front of them with a style and standard of football never before witnessed in the eleven years of the competition, and this game is no different.

Sir Alex Ferguson will tell you this particular Arsenal vintage, no matter what the record books say, are not a great side, that they drew too many matches to be considered era-defining. He was certainly never shy of voicing that theory to journalists on the Manchester beat.

Yes, for sheer drama, Manchester United's Treble season was probably the most thrilling of the Premier League's formative years, but that was down to so many games and situations that looked beyond rescue yet were somehow salvaged; of individual performances that still rank among the highest seen in the English game, of fleeting moments of fate that defined a campaign.

Teddy Sheringham once said there was no greater sight in football than United chasing a game, that adrenalin-soaked defiance that never saw them surrender an inch. And maybe he is right in many respects.

Arsenal, though, were beautiful to watch, truly beautiful. Even before I had the pleasure of researching this book and watching hours of footage from The Invincibles season, I could play moves out in my mind that came to embody everything for which Arsenal stood.

Jens Lehmann bowls the ball out to Ashley Cole who makes ground to the halfway line before feeding Robert Pires down the left. Pires and his unique 'ten-to-two' gait teases defenders across before a ball speared into Dennis Bergkamp.

Time freezes, the world stops, Bergkamp's brain is fizzing with angles, geometry, measured degrees of perfection. Thierry Henry is alive to every possibility and has already taken the stride that will defeat his marker. The ball runs true, never a millimetre's deviation, and Henry is on it, supreme controlled menace, one touch to balance, the second to score with either fury or finesse, it matters not which.

It is how I see it still. It is no particular game, no particular goal, just an image of majesty that Arsenal produced with wonderful regularity throughout the season, from August through to May. It brings people to their feet, even in the cramped confines of a press box that is barely fit for purpose but that nobody wants to leave. It is not just the goals, it is the complete domination of the opposition, the harmony of movement and thought, the pleasure of redefining what the game could represent.

Arsène Wenger had driven this quest for what counts as the closest thing to a perfect season in football. In other sports you can quantify perfection in statistics; the 147 in snooker, the nine-dart finish, the 300-point game in bowling. In the Premier League, an unbeaten campaign is the pinnacle, one that Wenger believed was possible – all he had to do was convince his players.

In his foreword to Amy Lawrence's excellent story of that season, *Invincible*, Wenger explained his thought process. 'I knew I had a special team in 2003–04. It had always been my dream to go through a season without losing, even though it is not a normal ambition.

'What made that aspiration so special is that I strive for perfection. I have always wanted to do my job as well as I can. At the end of each season, I ask myself, have I done the maximum with this team? Nobody can truly measure that, only you know deeply if there was more to give.

'So I always admired the idea to win a championship without losing a game, because you cannot do much better. You think then you have done your job in a perfect way. To win, taking every drop out of the team, and pushing them as far as they can, is the utmost achievement. That's why you can never release the concentration, focus or commitment.'

Belief was the key. Arsenal had scaled the heights before but could not sustain, not like United who had won three Premier League titles in a row and would go on to do it again under Ferguson, an almost superhuman accomplishment and testament to their mental durability.

Perhaps that was what was lacking at Highbury, an ability to regenerate the hunger season after season. The players felt Wenger had ramped up the pressure to such an extent in his quest for an unbeaten campaign the previous year that they had wilted and were unable to replicate the form that had taken them to the title in 2001–02.

How do you change that mindset? The answer is multi-faceted, but it helps if you recruit the kind of player who strengthens not only the team but the core mentality. Jens Lehmann was such a player.

Wenger's philosophy was always to sign young players and develop them, taking the raw material and nurturing it in the Arsenal way. Rarely did he deviate from that course, to the point of fanaticism. He made an exception for Lehmann.

The German was thirty-three, and had the experience of winning a European trophy at Schalke in a ten-year spell before leaving for Milan and then returning home to win the Bundesliga with Borussia Dortmund. This was a player unlikely to be daunted by the Arsenal dressing room and almost certain to instil his own intensity of personality on the squad.

Intense probably does not do Lehmann justice. There was an almost manic quality that radiated off him both in games and on the training pitch and that saw him clash with virtually every player at one stage or another when, in his opinion, they were failing to match his exacting standards. It could have alienated the squad, instead it galvanised them, as Patrick Vieira explains in *Invincible*: 'Jens was a nightmare, but he brought something.

'Before, our mentality was at one level and when Jens came, it just went higher. Jens argued with every single player in training because he wants you to get concentrated, he wants you to work hard, he wants you to win. Jens will not accept a player giving seventy or eighty per cent, he expects one hundred per cent.

'Jens brought us to a different level in terms of the winning mentality. He was never happy, always complaining, but he was a really good guy.'

If Lehmann and Bergkamp were relative veterans in their thirties, the remainder of the squad were developing and maturing together, comfortable in their environment, all with several years at Arsenal under their belts, all at home with the demands of the Premier League. Vieira, Pires and Bergkamp had all signed long-term deals in the summer of 2003 to cement the belief this was a club in the ascendancy, no matter what United could throw at them.

And on 21 September, the full fury of Old Trafford came their way.

Six games into the season, nobody is even contemplating the thought of a faultless campaign, let alone discussing it. How could you when Ruud van Nistelrooy is standing over the ball 12 yards from Lehmann's goal, a penalty kick in the last minute to decide a game which, in its last fifteen minutes, had been snarling and spiteful.

Vieira was long gone, a second yellow card for kicking out at van Nistelrooy; the fact his right foot did not come within three feet of the Dutchman meant nothing, the striker's exaggerated reaction somehow convincing referee Stephen Bennett there had been contact. Such was Vieira's fury at the injustice that Roy Keane felt compelled to act as peacemaker, ushering his fiercest rival away, a consoling hand on the back of his neck. Keane knew.

And here was van Nistelrooy, all awkward elbows and looks of pained innocence, about to bring an end to Arsenal's unbeaten run and take United to the top of the table. He tamps the penalty spot down with his foot, places and then replaces the ball before a six-step run-up and a thrash of his right foot sends Lehmann the wrong way but hammers against the bar.

In that instant, the seed of immortality is sown. Arsenal will face other challenges over the next eight months but to have endured this, to have come through unscathed, says much about the growing bond of belief. Unscathed, however, is a relative term. Martin Keown's wild leap into the back of van Nistelrooy on the final whistle was always going to attract the attention of the Football Association's disciplinary department, but the skirmishes at the end saw a rash of charges, six for Arsenal and three for United.

Wenger, who also saw the club charged with failing to control their players, was forced into a grudging apology after his chairman, Peter Hill-Wood, publicly condemned the actions at Old Trafford. As apologies go, it was delivered through gritted teeth and you sensed there may have been a very different message given to his players, one that focused on Arsenal against the world.

Certainly, they were not distracted either by events at Old Trafford or by the glacial process of the FA's investigations. Off the back of the draw at United, Arsenal beat Newcastle United, Liverpool and Chelsea while playing regal football. If Ferguson had perfected the art of the siege mentality in his years at United, Wenger was refining it with a touch of Gallic psychology. As midfielder Gilberto Silva explained to Amy Lawrence, 'In football, you are not allowed to lose your focus at any time.

'In the previous season, the crucial moment was in Bolton when we threw away the game. After that, we couldn't return to our best, it seemed like everyone forgot about playing football. But that game at Old Trafford showed a different character, as if we had learned from the recent past. We didn't want that to happen again.'

Old Trafford was too early in the season to be a turning point. What it did prove to the players collectively was that there was nothing to fear, that a United side even with Keane, Ryan Giggs and Rio Ferdinand in the ranks was no longer the benchmark to be admired and regarded with awe; Arsenal could not only compete, they could also shine in comparison.

It also helps if you can call on, in my opinion, the finest player to grace the Premier League, not just in the timeframe of this book but in its thirty-year history. Alan Shearer was the goal-scorer supreme, Wayne Rooney a force of nature, Cristiano Ronaldo shimmered for a brief time and Keane was always a magnificent presence. But Henry? Henry simply bestrode the English game like it was his birthright.

Gone was the nervous, awkward twenty-one-year-old who had been tracked and ignored by every one of Europe's elite as he struggled at Juventus who, ridiculously, played him as a winger – every one, that is, except Arsenal. Wenger knew him, of course, from their time together at Monaco, but by 1999, Henry's confidence, the one thing that defined him as a player, had been destroyed by Italian football.

'He had lost something and basically, that was belief,' Wenger recalled as he reflected on Henry's arrival. 'People in life arrive early at a good level and don't move too much because they don't push themselves. You can be a professional football player, but do you want to discover something more? Do you want to explore really what football can give you?'

Henry needed only to hear those words, as he admitted, 'Arsène changed my life. He gave me an opportunity to shine, and I can never thank him enough for that. I wasn't a centre forward if you watch me play but Arsène gave me that freedom. He makes you realise how good you can be, he allowed me to express myself.'

And what an expression of insouciant brilliance. There was arrogance, but why not? When you are as good as Henry, then arrogance is a weapon in your armoury, a coruscating self-belief that intimidates the opposition before they have even set foot on the pitch: give me the ball, I am the one that can make things happen, I can change destiny.

You see it sometimes in his goal celebrations, a simple tight-lipped nodding, an understanding that this is simply what Henry DOES; why would you expect any different? Yet at other times, there is the guttural war cry of acclaim, as if even Henry himself has been astonished at what the combination of mental and physical perfection can deliver.

The mere numbers will never do him justice or even come close to painting the full picture of his impact on English football. He brought something that those of us fortunate enough to cover the Premier League had never witnessed and is difficult to quantify. Was it his athleticism? His grace with the ball at his feet? His pace and power? His appreciation of space and time? His transformative anger? In the Premier League's first decade, some had a few of those qualities but no one player was complete, not like Henry.

He was not always comfortable to be around as a journalist. The merest suggestion of unfair criticism would prompt a demand to the Arsenal media team to supply a telephone number for the perceived offender, followed by further demands to explain and justify what had been written. There was also the time on a Champions League trip when his finger-jabbing anger at a reporter delayed a flight until Henry could be cajoled back to his seat.

Yet to sit with him in his more considered moments, generally when the tape recorders were put away, was to witness an athlete who realised what he could do but not always how. I was lucky to sit next to him at a tribute dinner some years after he retired and asked him about several of his goals and performances in true fan-boy fashion.

Whether it was modesty or the impossibility of self-analysis, in Henry's opinion, it came down to instinct. Often, he said, he could not even think why he had been in a certain position to receive a pass, it was never a tactical decision to drop deep or fade wide, something within him simply told him where to stand or move.

'Sometimes, I see myself from above when I am on a pitch,' he said. 'When that happens, I am not really in control, I am just moving without really thinking, that is the only way I can explain it.'

The Invincibles were an astonishing collection of players peaking at exactly the same time, driven by a belief that history was theirs for the taking, and with a bond of trust and understanding that could not be broken. Yet, as Sir Alex Ferguson admitted years after the pain of playing second best to Arsenal had subsided, 'The change in Arsenal was the reinvention of Thierry Henry, no question.'

Even great players recognise there is often someone special alongside them, that presence who can alter the course of a season, even in one game. Manchester United, in those early years of the Premier League, turned to Eric Cantona when the team were troubled. Alan Shearer was as reliable a talisman for Blackburn as the League had seen to that point and, after Cantona left the arena, Roy Keane took his mantle.

In the space of six days in April, Arsenal had never needed Henry more.

On 3 April, the Treble beckoned as Wenger's side faced the prospect of burying the ghost of 1999 with an FA Cup semi-final against United back at Villa Park before the second leg of their Champions League quarter-final against Chelsea at Highbury, with Arsenal taking a valuable away goal from the first-leg 1–1 draw. It was there before them, a tableau that demanded excellence and conviction but one that should have been within their grasp.

Yet, there was nothing. Henry had been rested for the FA Cup and Arsenal looked lethargic in every area of the pitch, lumpen almost. United did not even have to be at their best to beat them – courtesy of a single Paul Scholes goal – such was the paucity of Arsenal's performance.

Three days later, a season that had offered so much was down to the sole target of the Premier League, as Chelsea, showing for the first time at this level that Roman Abramovich's billions were transformative, relentlessly ground down the Gunners, Wayne Bridge's winner three minutes from the end bringing Arsenal to their knees.

As the players trudged through the mixed zone on the side of the Stamford Bridge pitch, there was a fatigue to them evidenced not just in their slumped shoulders, but in their eyes. It was the thousand-yard stare of men who, prior to that week, had not tasted defeat since October (to Dynamo Kyiv in the Champions League) but now saw the lifeblood of their season ebbing away.

There could be no respite as Liverpool, the final name in Arsenal's trio of challengers, arrived at Highbury on Good Friday. After forty-five minutes, the splinter of Villa Park that became a fracture at the Bridge was now an open wound, as Arsenal returned to their Highbury dressing room trailing 2–1 with only an Henry effort sandwiched between Sami Hyypiä and Michael Owen goals to show for their efforts.

Arsenal players of the time talk of feeling broken in those fifteen minutes, or, as Henry puts it, 'I felt the stadium stopped breathing.' There is no anger, just despondency, and a sense of futility, as if everything of the last eight months amounted to zero. Still, Wenger sensed there was still an element of resolve – and it came in the redoubtable form of Martin Keown.

Keown only made eight full appearances that season yet was never a peripheral figure, with his constant chiding, enthusiasm and commitment in training never allowing more illustrious teammates to give less than everything they possessed. Now, he asked Wenger for permission to speak. It may not have been Churchillian, but it was effective. 'There was a sense of us feeling sorry for ourselves and everything's going down the pan.

'So I said, "Look, fellas. We're feeling pretty sorry for ourselves. This is the best group of players I've ever played with. If we get that first goal then this ground, this crowd, are just waiting for us, and it will turn on its head."'

Keown's words resonate with Henry. 'Highbury, in those hard moments, gave us everything: life, power, will, desire. All I can remember is me coming out of the tunnel, just wanting to get back out on the field and rectify what had been done.'

Henry helps prompt the equaliser, feeding Freddie Ljungberg whose first-time pass falls for Pires to time his break into the Liverpool area and prod the ball home. It was a goal of quality and refinement – but one which pales in comparison with what was to follow.

I would argue that it is not the greatest goal Henry ever scored. My personal favourite is the flick-up and volley against United four years earlier, probably helped by the fact I was directly in line in the press box as the ball arced over Fabien Barthez and Highbury rose as one to Henry's genius. However, I am willing to concede this was a goal that nobody else on Earth could have scored at that time.

Of the whole Liverpool team, only Owen is behind Henry when he picks up the ball level with the centre circle, yet in the space of just a few devastating seconds, he has held off

Didi Hamann, reduced Jamie Carragher to a puppet with his strings cut before a finish of such delicious precision seems to bend the rules of geometry to his own will. With it, all the fear and anguish that shrouded Arsenal was lifted in a joyous acclamation of his genius.

Words – both those of any journalist and even Henry himself – cannot truly do the goal justice. 'When I took that ball, I told myself I was going to go, no matter what. When I scored, it felt like we all scored, it felt like everything came back.'

For Wenger, it is a testament to what he always believed was in the gift of his team. 'You can go very quickly into a confidence crisis,' he recalls in Gabriel Clarke's superb documentary *Invincible*. 'Every defeat makes it more difficult to repair the damage done. But the more the dream looks impossible, the more it can strengthen your motivation.'

Henry's third and Arsenal's fourth is a mere adornment, it was THAT goal that etched the conviction back in their cause and put Chelsea, who were chasing hardest, in their place. A draw and a win in their next two games meant Wenger's men only needed a point – at White Hart Lane, of all places – to secure the title with four games to spare.

Do NOT celebrate, was the police warning, should Arsenal clinch the league at the home of their hated North London rivals. To deny that explosion of joy when the final whistle blew on a 2–2 draw was a wretched request and would always be ignored.

From the moment the Premier League was secured, Wenger admits he said very little to his team, except to remind them that destiny was now in their own hands. He felt no cause for concern, the trust in his players was absolute, the perfection he sought not some elusive, ephemeral fantasy but a concrete reality.

Immortality was assured with draws against Birmingham

City and Portsmouth followed by a victory at Fulham and then, on a glorious sunlit day at Highbury, goals from Henry and Vieira saw off Leicester. The statistic of twenty-six wins and twelve draws is now forever etched in football history, but there was always so much more than soulless facts to Arsenal's season.

In Gabriel Clarke's documentary, Wenger describes himself as a 'pragmatic romantic', where the craving for victory may be all-consuming but must carry with it more than just three points. As he explained, 'We are in the entertainment business and the ground mark is to win. But that is not enough. You have to give more, to go deeper in what the game can give people.

'To get more than just the individual expression of a player or the collective expression of a team, to transform it into art.

'You can say it's naïve but you need to give inspiration to people, to get them out of their hard daily lives. I just want them to sit in their seat and think, "Unbelievable."'

19

Thirty Years Later ...

Let's start with the numbers.

Until 2025, the Premier League television deal is worth over £10 billion, with international rights worth more than the domestic for the first time. The Premier League champions will earn £176 million for each of those three years, with even those relegated teams picking up more than £100 million.

The last analysis of the Premier League's reach overseen by Ernst & Young concluded that 3.2 billion people worldwide watched at least one Premier League match in the season 2019–20, while 878 million homes globally had access to games. In the same season, 528,000 tourists travelled to the United Kingdom with the sole intention of attending a Premier League match.

Over two hundred countries have bought the rights to Premier League games, while players from 113 different countries have played at least one Premier League game. In the Euro 2020 tournament, the Premier League had 119 players, the most of any league represented.

Thirty years after those first nine games kicked off on 15 August 1992, the Premier League is not only a sporting behemoth, it is a tool of geopolitical power, a glittering prize for sovereign wealth funds and a home for billionaires from around the globe, all desperate for a share of its reflected glory.

It is, at once, both an archetype of capitalist excess and a body that largely relies on socialist principles of collective bargaining, even if that ethic is being eroded by the demands of the very richest of its brethren.

Around the globe, it is viewed with such fear and envy that people have colluded in an attempt to either denude the league of its power or share a place at the highest table. Nothing, though, has disturbed its dominance of the globe's football landscape because nothing delivers as vividly and as regularly as the Premier League.

Whatever the marketing men, the advertising executives and commercial mandarins would have you believe, the football the Premier League produces is not a 'product', even though it is too often packaged that way. It's a living, breathing ferment of emotions played out before devoted audiences in stadia that are regularly 98 per cent full and on television screens, tablets, laptops, PCs and mobile phones across the world.

Its development has been breathtaking, yet, at its heart, the game is no different. The football fans who rose to acknowledge the first goal scored by Brian Deane in 1992 are the same who rise to acclaim a strike by Kevin De Bruyne or Mo Salah or Cristiano Ronaldo thirty years later.

I stand by the advice given to me by mentor and former *News of the World* sports editor, Bill Bateson, when I joined the paper. He said, 'Never forget what football is all about. It's not about money and men in suits, it's about mud on boots.' And while, as Alan Shearer points out in the foreword to this book, there's precious little mud left in the Premier League, the essence of Bill's words remains as true now as it did when I was taking my first steps in the industry.

There has never been an open-top bus ride for a balance sheet, but hundreds of thousands will take to the street to welcome heroes arriving home with silverware, be it in the streets of Manchester, the red halves of North London and Merseyside or even, unexpectedly, Leicester.

What else can stir the emotions like Martin Tyler's guttural 'Aguerooooooo'? Or Wayne Rooney's overhead goal against Manchester City? Or Cristiano Ronaldo seemingly redefining the laws of physics with a dead-ball strike whose perfection was honed by hours on the training ground yet was scored with such swaggering nonchalance?

I recall a conversation with former Premier League chief executive Richard Scudamore shortly after he had signed yet another stratospheric television rights deal. We were at an end-of-season awards dinner and I, in my naivety, mused that there had to be a point where a financial ceiling was reached.

Scudamore looked at me with almost pity at my innocence and, yes, my stupidity. 'If you continually give people what they want and even more, they will always pay,' he explained. 'The newspaper industry will eventually die out because you're expecting people to pay more and more for something that doesn't really get any better.

'And when the industry does try to innovate by going digital behind a paywall, you're then asking people to pay for content you've previously given away for free. It's a flawed model and one that will be the death of newspapers, possibly not in our lifetime, but certainly somewhere in the future.

'The Premier League makes a lot of money, but it also gives the clubs lots of money. They then give players and managers lots of money and, eventually, you are able to pay for the people who are the very best in the world at what they do. When you are delivering the very best, then people will always pay to watch that.'

From a self-confessed newspaper man at heart, Scudamore's words sounded horribly fatalistic as far as my industry was concerned, but as with so many other things, he could not have been more prescient in his view.

The Premier League has delivered. From Ferguson to Wenger to Mourinho to Guardiola and Klopp; from Cantona to Henry to Rooney to Silva to Kane, the consistency of excellence has been unremitting. And if there is ugliness in the shape of boardroom battles, of existential threats and armed conflict forcing change, it is always outweighed by the brilliance of the drama unfolding on the pitch.

So how do you even begin to plot the trajectory of the Premier League's rise to its standing on its thirtieth anniversary? In 1999, I didn't think there would ever be a sight more thrilling than Manchester United's pursuit of the Treble and all its incredible twists. To me, that is still the greatest story of the first three decades.

But then Arsenal under Wenger redefined the way in which the English game could be played and even Sir Alex Ferguson was forced to – albeit temporarily – admit defeat. Would Arsenal's dominance have continued without the arrival of Roman Abramovich and then José Mourinho? I suspect only for another year at most, given the financially sapping demands of the move from Highbury to the Emirates Stadium.

Abramovich's billions changed the very fabric of the game to such an extent that everything should be viewed through the prism of his arrival on English shores. The famous David Dein quote is always worth recalling at this point – 'Roman Abramovich has parked his Russian tank in our front garden and is firing £50 notes at us' – because it was a move that disfigured the Premier League.

Supporters went from wanting their club to play like Arsenal to urging them to spend money like Chelsea, and if that meant José Mourinho's ruthless efficiency rather than Wenger's football for the soul, it seemed like a sacrifice many fans were willing to take.

It was around this time that I began to lose my passion for the Premier League. Mourinho was always a story, always a headline, but there was something about his cynicism and self-adoration that seemed particularly unappealing. He wasn't a villain, far from it, and there was much to admire in his ability to extract every ounce of talent from the likes of Frank Lampard, Didier Drogba and John Terry.

But there was still something in Mourinho the man that smacked of an arrogance never seen before in the Premier League. I have been fortunate and privileged to be invited into the training-ground offices of Ferguson, Wenger, Gerard Houllier and many other managers over the years. There are always mementos of past triumphs, the odd photograph and certainly some reminder of a family from whom they are too often separated by the demands of the game.

Mourinho's office at Cobham, however, was nothing short of a shrine to himself. Every wall was adorned with images of him holding trophies or being mobbed by his players. The only books I could see were about Mourinho, the magazines scattered on a coffee table all had him on the front cover. It was a masterclass in the art of the ego, of one man's enduring love for himself, Narcissus made flesh in the heart of Surrey's stockbroker belt.

At the same time, Old Trafford was being torn apart by the protests against the Glazer family, who completed their takeover of Manchester United in the summer of 2005, heaping millions of pounds' worth of debt on a club that had previously been debt-free and destroying any lingering trust between board and fan base. For years the fight continued and, even now, the ramifications are still being felt, with protests heard again towards the end of the 2021–22 season and into the next.

That same story would be retold on Merseyside less than eighteen months later as another club disturbed by the prospect of continually being outspent by Chelsea would suffer at the hands of new American owners.

Tom Hicks and George Gillett brought Liverpool to their knees, buying the club on the cheap with a mountain of borrowed money only for their plans at investment to be destroyed by the combination of a global economic crash and a complete breakdown in their business and personal relationship.

It was a dispiriting time to be covering the game – England even failed to qualify for the 2008 European Championship – so when the opportunity arose to give up life as a reporter and become sports editor back at the *News of the World*, I did not hesitate.

Not for a moment did I regret that decision, but being once removed from the day-to-day coverage made me realise the one thing I missed was the atmosphere of match day and, more specifically, just being among football fans every Saturday afternoon or midweek night.

There have been times when finding yourself among fans was far from comforting: being chased through Newcastle's Bigg Market after being wrongly identified as Manchester United supporters, being caught up in running battles between England's hardcore and Italian police on the streets of Rome in 1997 or being abused more than a few times in press boxes up and down the country are not things I would recommend.

Yet the passion and humour of supporters is something I did miss and should never be either overlooked or underestimated for the part that it has played in lifting the Premier League to the global status it currently enjoys.

There are huge games across Europe that attract the same fervour, whether in Italy, Spain or France, but dig deeper and the loyalty of the English football fan shames their continental cousins. Mid-table games in Europe are too often met with a degree of apathy among supporters; in the Premier League they are invariably as close to sell-outs as makes no difference.

By and large, football fans in the Premier League keep their clubs honest. There will always be tribalism where supporters turn a blind eye to even the most obvious failings – and Newcastle supporters' tolerance of Saudi Arabia's failings in terms of human rights stands as the latest incarnation of that – but fans' voices make a difference.

I am writing this final chapter on the first anniversary of one of the darkest days in English football history, when six Premier League clubs decided they would happily destroy the structure of the English game by signing up to the European Super League and a closed shop of greed.

The Premier League itself seemed powerless to stop Manchester United, Manchester City, Arsenal, Tottenham, Liverpool and Chelsea from simply removing themselves and joining the two Milan clubs, Atletico and Real Madrid and Barcelona in an ersatz competition between those clubs who presumed their riches made them impervious to either criticism or common decency.

In fact, Scudamore – again, in a moment of foresight – had seen this coming even before he exited the Premier League three years earlier. His brilliance as an administrator was convincing the clubs they were always stronger as a collective bargaining unit, that a unified front would ensure the smaller clubs would not be left by the wayside if broadcasters were allowed to cherry pick the clubs and fixtures that simply garnered the biggest audiences.

His nineteen-year reign at Premier League headquarters

was a triumph and, in my opinion, he should be judged as one of the most influential figures of the last three decades alongside Ferguson, Abramovich and Sheikh Mansour. The domestic and global television deals he negotiated were the envy of every other league in Europe and, for the vast majority of his time, Scudamore kept the clubs happy with his commercial prowess while maintaining the collective unity needed to maintain that balance.

Once the twenty chairmen agreed to a greater share of the international rights being distributed to the bigger clubs in 2018, that balance was lost. A thread had successfully been pulled and the Big Six would no longer be satisfied until the whole golden garment had unravelled.

Who could stop them if the game's authorities were emasculated? Fans. Only fans.

If supporters in Madrid, Turin, Milan and Barcelona simply shrugged, English fans rose up in a show of civil disobedience that shamed their European counterparts. Within hours, protests around grounds became acts of deafening defiance as the guilty clubs were forced to cancel matches and offer grovelling apologies for their ill-conceived actions and dreadful misreading of supporter loyalty. Within days, the very foundations of the Super League were destroyed by fans who shamed those at the top of their clubs.

It was more than just an echo of the protests that forced Hicks and Gillett out of Anfield, or the screams of disgust at the way Mike Ashley treated Newcastle, or even the uprising at Old Trafford that saw previously loyal fans turn their backs on the Glazers and even Ferguson to form a new club that vowed never to betray its roots; the destruction of the Super League (for now) was the purest form of supporter power and a recognition that fans were the ultimate guardians of the game's soul.

With that power, though, comes a brutality that can be uncomfortable even for those of us who believe in the absolute right of supporter opinion. The treatment of Wenger is the perfect case in point, where the ugliness of the factionalism within the Arsenal fan base obscured everything the manager had sacrificed for the club: his marriage, time with his family, anything approaching a normally balanced life, all in the name of footballing success and beauty.

To see Wenger hounded out after what he had brought to the English game, after raising standards to such a height that even Ferguson was left trailing in his wake, felt tawdry and wrong. It also felt like he was a victim of an era; that, no matter how deep his conviction towards playing the football of his principles, he would always have been outmanoeuvred by a pound note. It was the death of dreaming.

I wish Wenger could have left on a high, the same way his old foe in Manchester had done in 2013. Ferguson's departure from Old Trafford should be judged through the same lens as Abramovich's arrival in London: an era-defining event that changed the power dynamic of the Premier League and English football at the highest level.

For the seven years before he finally announced his retirement, Ferguson had underlined his genius by largely fending off even those rivals bolstered by untold wealth, reducing Abramovich's Chelsea to an almost comedic level of boom-and-bust managerial recruitment while Abu Dhabi royals could only look on with frustration as he kept the noisy neighbours of Manchester City relatively quiet. Five Premier League titles and another Champions League crown proved that success could not merely be bought, it also had to be earned.

There may be a stand at Old Trafford named in his honour, but it feels like there should be something extra, something significant to enshrine him in Premier League folklore more than just in mere record books. Naming the trophy after him is something that I have debated with Premier League chiefs, especially as there is no longer a single title sponsor. Would the Sir Alex Ferguson Trophy not be a fitting testimony to his genius?

I would give it to him simply as a thank-you for the part he played in the greatest Premier League game of my reporting career. It was 29 September 2001, and United were 3–0 down at White Hart Lane at half-time – and it could have been a lot more given Tottenham's superiority. Apparently, there was little said at the break, just some withering looks and a few choice reminders of why a club of Manchester United's stature would not tolerate such feeble surrender.

The second half was the greatest single forty-five minutes it has been my pleasure to cover. United, in riotous full flow, absolutely decimated Spurs with five unanswered goals and the kind of barely concealed fury that mirrored their manager. It was a life-affirming reminder of the privilege of a reporter's job.

I still do not think I have seen anything to match that, either in the flesh or as a television viewer, although the rivalry between Manchester City and Liverpool, each pushing the other to such heights and feats of excellence, has at times come close.

Gary Neville has distinguished himself as a pundit and analyst of great insight, but never has he uttered a truer word than when he proclaimed that City and Liverpool produce the finest football the Premier League has ever witnessed and that Pep Guardiola and Jürgen Klopp are taking the English game to levels that sometimes defy belief.

To know that you need to be within touching distance of 100 points to win the title is astonishing, as is the knowledge that a century of goals is now well within the grasp of both clubs. But, again, it is more than just dry statistics; it is the ethos of the way the game is demanded by both managers that has elevated the spectacle.

Thirty years on, is English football healthier now than at the advent of the Premier League? And what parameters should be used to make that judgement.

Financially, the answer would appear obvious. How can any league that annually guarantees its clubs a share of £3 billion worth of revenue be anything but in rude health? Well, try telling that to Leeds United fans who saw their club go into administration, a move that stemmed from ruinous spending and financial gambles that backfired horrifically. Or those supporters of Bolton Wanderers who, after many successful seasons in the Premier League, suckling at its generous teat, were just days away from going out of business. Or Blackpool, Oldham and Swindon, who have briefly tasted Premier League glory only to fade away into varying degrees of obscurity.

The Premier League comes at you hard and fast. One poor managerial appointment, two badly judged transfer windows in succession, and even the biggest clubs or those with a long-standing Premier League pedigree can find themselves in a world of pain that even a £100 million softener cannot dilute. When even some of the most successful clubs never come close to turning a profit, what hope for those who are gambling on paying wages that outstrip income just to survive in the promised land?

So, while financial security is often an illusion, where else can football be adjudged healthier thanks to the Premier League?

One area where, undoubtedly, our game has benefited these past three decades is in the level of facilities enjoyed by players and supporters alike. Training grounds are sumptuous, more akin to seven-star health spas, with their sleeping pods, recovery pools, state-of-the-art gyms and personalised fitness plans, not to mention medical staff, masseurs and player liaison officers on hand to provide a twenty-four-hour concierge service. Does any player yearn for the days of a bacon butty and a mug of builder's tea before training? I doubt it.

The stadia are stellar, from Tottenham's architectural monolith through to Brentford's beautifully designed new ground, nestling perfectly between the elevated section of the M4 and the Thames, discreet, highly functional and as worthy of a place in the Premier League as Old Trafford, the Etihad or Anfield.

No fan need ever feel the sickening warmth of urine soak the back of their legs or queue for a dismal burger at half-time. Some might tell you this is all too sterile, too saccharine, but never believe them because their craving for nostalgia fails to mention the fear of crushing or the threat of violence which scarred too many match days for some of us.

And what is the price we pay for modern life not being rubbish? We look away when oligarchs, billionaires and crown princes arrive, desperate to believe their presence is based on fun, philanthropy or just a desire to immerse themselves in a league where they can be worshipped simply for spending and where success on the pitch masks a deeper question of ethics, be they moral or financial.

Yet it is telling that the last great act of the Premier League's twenty-ninth anniversary was the departure of the man who probably changed the English game more than any other. Roman Abramovich, whether he intended to or not, altered the conversation exponentially yet also acted as a full stop. His exit from Stamford Bridge saw English football confront topics it had chosen to ignore for too long, although why it took slaughter in Ukraine to prompt that confrontation makes for an uncomfortable position for those of us who, while never believing Abramovich was a force for good, still happily went along for the ride.

The Premier League itself is planning no major celebrations for the anniversary, choosing to look forward rather than back, concentrating on community events with their clubs to honour thirty years of achievements at a local level. It is a sign of the relentless nature of the beast that it feels no particular need to reflect on three decades of astonishing success, not when there is still new ground to break via global streaming services or fresh deals to sign.

Of course, there is a sense of pride at the endless theatre and magnificent spectacle the Premier League provides and also the satisfaction of its commercial might that shows no sign of being diluted any time soon.

The Greed is Good League, as proclaimed by Brian Glanville all those years ago? Well, perhaps. But there is so much more to it than bald, financial muscle.

There are still dreams, still devotion, still undying love for the players and managers. There is still escapism and adventure, still a chance that someone carved from the same (comparatively) modest stone as Leicester City can upset Pep's City or Klopp's Liverpool. That the team at the bottom can always surprise the team at the top.

There is still beauty and joy to be had, unalloyed moments of inexplicable pleasure that confound and delight in equal measure. For all the marketing, crass commercial exploitation, hubris and hyperbole, there is still a purity to eleven against eleven, ours against yours, and may the best team – not the richest – triumph.

It has been a privilege to both chronicle and witness the rise and rise of the Premier League. It truly has been a whole new ball game.

Acknowledgements

It was an honour to be asked to write this book but also a reminder that I must be fast approaching veteran stage given my journalism career started before the advent of the Premier League and has been dominated by its presence even after I changed roles and started working as a media consultant.

The job of recalling and researching this thirty-year journey was made so much easier by all the people who spent hours of their time to be interviewed and put the meat on the bones. Without them, this labour of love would have been simply a labour.

I am also especially indebted to journalistic colleagues who have trodden a similar path in chronicling some of the major characters and events of the Premier League years, albeit with far more eloquence than I could ever muster. To Simon Hughes for *Men In White Suits* and Amy Lawrence for *Invincible*, both of whom generously allowed me to plunder their work where there were gaps that needed filling.

A hat tip also to Gabriel Clarke's superb documentary for Amazon, *Arsène Wenger: Invincible*, which gave me a detailed understanding of one of the most significant figures in this book (and far beyond). I've lost count of the number of times I've watched it yet still marvel at some of the football Wenger's team played.

To everybody at Little, Brown – Ed Wood, Nithya Rae and Linda Silverman – thank you for your guidance, patience and expertise. Also, to Adam Hopkins at Story Films whose hard work provided the foundations for the book and helped make my task simpler.

To a few people who gave such fantastic insight into the origins of the Premier League. David Dein, Andy Melvin, Geoff Shreeves and Richard Keys were all there on the ground floor of football history and they generously gave up their time to reminisce and put me straight on a few key moments. Chaps, lunch is on me.

Working in football journalism has been the greatest job I could ever have experienced, and growing up with the Premier League has been wonderful. To friends who made it such fun along the way – Lee Clayton, Ollie Holt, Paul Hayward, Matt Dickins, Andy Dunn and so many others – thanks for all the memories of marvellous matches, great nights and amazing trips. To cover them all alongside you was an honour.

Finally, to the late, great Bill Bateson who constantly reminded me when I was in danger of forgetting – 'It's all about mud on boots, son. Never lose sight of that.'

Index